RM 13|-

46

CONQUESTS & DISCOVERIES OF
OF
HENRY THE NAVIGATOR

PORTRAIT OF THE INFANTE DOM HENRIQUE
(HENRY THE NAVIGATOR)

From a miniature of the fifteenth century.—*Azurara, Chronique de la Conquête de Guinée, B.N. Paris, ms. Port.* 41, *fol.* 5

CONQUESTS & DISCOVERIES
OF
HENRY THE NAVIGATOR

BEING THE
CHRONICLES OF AZURARA
*Portuguese Navigators & Colonizers of the
Fifteenth & Sixteenth Centuries*

edited by
VIRGINIA DE CASTRO E ALMEIDA

with a Preface by
MARSHAL LYAUTEY

translated by Bernard Miall

LONDON
GEORGE ALLEN & UNWIN LTD
MUSEUM STREET

Translated from the first French edition of *Chroniques de Gomes Eannes de Azurara*, in the series "Les Grands Navigateurs et Colons Portugais du XVe et du XVIe Siècles: Anthologie des Écrits de l'Epoque par Virginia de Castro e Almeida." Éditions Duchartre, Paris, 1934

FIRST PUBLISHED IN ENGLISH, 1936

I dedicate this book to His Excellency the Secretary-General to the Portuguese Ministry for Foreign Affairs, Senhor Luiz Teixeira de Sampayo, and to the Permanent Delegate for Portugal to the League of Nations, Dr. Augusto de Vasconcellos.

VIRGINIA DE CASTRO E ALMEIDA

Paris, November 1933

CONTENTS

The Chronicle of the Discovery of Guinea

ILLUSTRATIONS

PREFACE

SENHORA VIRGINIA DE CASTRO E AL-
MEIDA has asked me to introduce to her readers
a work which is destined to make the heroic colonial
epopée of Portugal more widely known to the general
public.

To this wish of hers I very gladly accede, although
my compatriots have but recently had occasion to
admire the colonizing achievements of her country,
as they passed through the halls of those delightful
palaces which constituted, in the International
Colonial Exhibition, the instructive and suggestive
Lusitanian section.

I can only repeat what I said, with complete
conviction, when I made my inaugural speech on the
day when these pavilions opened their doors.

You are truly, I said, the pioneers of European
civilization on the shores of the Atlantic and Pacific
Oceans.

Yours is the land of the boldest navigators, and
you have left indelible traces of your passage and
your activities in every part of the earth; in America,
in Africa, in the Atlantic and Pacific Oceans, and in
the Far East.

When we consider that promontory in the south-
western corner of Europe which the Romans called
Sacrum, and which you, in the Latin fidelity of your
beautiful tongue, still know as *Sagres*, we see, on a wild
plateau which is battered by the ocean gales, the
ruins of a fortress of the fifteenth century, once the
home of a prince, Henry the Navigator, who combined

the disinterestedness of the scientist with the austerity of the saint.

In the shelter of these ancient walls were accumulated the manuscripts and the nautical charts which summed up the geographical knowledge of the West— there was the book of Marco Polo's travels, and there the charts which were drawn by Don Jayme de Mayorca (the Jewish maker of compasses) for the instruction of Portuguese officers.

How it thrills one to picture him leaning over the ramparts, eager to wrest its secrets from the unknown ocean!—this prince whom a manuscript in our national library depicts as clad in drugget, a black hood upon his head.

And it was from this centre, inspired by this flame, that so many navigators set out to reconnoitre the shores of Africa—so near, yet still so mysterious—little by little revealing to the world the lineaments and even the living faces of this Africa, which one cannot touch without loving.

And Madeira, the Azores, the Canaries—islands adorned with flowers and rich in fruits—they held the promises of those legends that told of the "Fortunate Isles."

As early as the middle of the fifteenth century you reached Cape Verde, and the captains of your caravels used to tell one another, as one of their company relates, that "Great is the desire of our Senhor the Infante to learn something of the Land of the Negroes, especially of the Nile; let us then go forth to conquer until we have found the Earthly Paradise."

I do not know whether they found the Earthly Paradise in Africa, but of one thing I am sure:

namely, the passionate interest of which one is conscious on comparing one with another your charts of the fifteenth century, on watching the gradual appearance on the coasts of Africa of the names which are now familiar to us all, and the location, from year to year, in their proper latitude, of those capes and river-mouths which are the sailor's landmarks.

And on these maps we see the points at which Diego Cão, in obedience to the command of King João the Second, erected those *padrões*, those stone columns which bear at the base the arms of the sovereign, and above it the cross of Christ.

I seem to remember that the Geographical Society of Lisbon has piously preserved one of these crosses, which was set up at the mouth of the Congo—that river which remained unknown until the last quarter of the nineteenth century.

We think of your Homer, Camoëns, singing in his *Lusiads* the exploits of your navigators.

We think of the Viceroyalty of the Indies—of Affonso d'Albuquerque—of Brazil, which you were the first to open up for civilization.

I myself have encountered you all along the coast of Morocco; at Mazagan, where your walls are still standing, and the fine monumental gates that bear the arms of your kings; in the old seaport of Safi; and at Mehedya, where your navigators foresaw the importance of what has to-day become the harbour to which Morocco has given my name.

These are noble titles to glory, of which your nation may lawfully be proud. But if, on turning from the past, I consider the many points of the globe above which your flag flies to-day—if, recalling the many great memories which are common to our two nations, I think of the ideal of your civilization, and your achievements overseas—I salute the colonizing efforts of Portugal as among not only the most glorious, but also the most efficacious and best deserving of the gratitude of humanity.

LYAUTEY

NOTE

THOSE portions of the text which are printed in close type are summaries of events whose records are too lengthy for unabridged translation; they serve to maintain continuity between those passages which are translated in full.

NOTES ON THE HISTORY
OF PORTUGAL

THE history of Portugal may be divided into three distinct periods, represented by three royal dynasties.

First Period: Dynasty of Burgundy, 1097–1383

At the beginning of the eighth century the Mohammedans of Africa invaded the Iberian peninsula, gaining complete possession of it, except for a small region in the mountains of the Asturias, where the Gothic prince Pelagius took refuge with some of his warriors. Pelagius opened the war against the Moors which was to continue for seven hundred years, until their final expulsion from the peninsula. This war saw the rise of the Christian kingdoms of the Asturias and Leon, Navarre, and Castile.

Towards the close of the eleventh century great numbers of foreign knights and squires came to engage in the service of Alfonso VI, King of Leon, Castile, and Galicia, for the holy war against the Infidels. Among them was Henry, Count of Burgundy, who, by the victorious battles which led him to the banks of the Tagus, won the hand of Teresa, daughter of Alfonso VI, and the government of the country of Portugal (embracing then little more than a portion of the northern region), which he soon made independent. His son, Affonso Henriques, became the first King of Portugal, and with him begins the dynasty of Burgundy.

This first period comprises the conquest of territory from the Moors; war against the Spaniards; the political and economic foundation and organization of the kingdom; and the delineation of the frontiers, which have remained unchanged until our own days.

Second Period: Dynasty of Aviz, 1383–1580

Discoveries, conquests, and colonization overseas; in Africa and the East; a period of intense external activity; the epic age of the mariner.

Third Period: Dynasty of Braganza, 1580–1853

The activities of the foregoing period had exhausted the nation. Moribund, it fell under the domination of Spain, which lasted for sixty years. Then Portugal shook off the Spanish yoke, and for twenty-seven years she fought for her independence. But then came the French invasions of Napoleon; war against the foreigner and civil war; and political disturbances, continuing until the middle of the nineteenth century.

The first and third periods belong to national history, but the second forms part of the history of the world.

It is too little known. The struggles which Portugal had to sustain and the difficulties which she had to overcome during the third period of her history did not leave her leisure to offer to the outside world a serious documentation of the maritime discoveries and conquests which opened a new era to the commerce, politics, and economy of the world.

A few foreign scholars and historians have dealt with this subject;[1] and numerous translations of the epic poem of Camoëns, the *Lusiads*, have appeared in

---

[1] See the excellent work by JEAN-PAUL ALAUX, *Vasco de Gama ou l'epopée des Portugais aux Indes.* Éditions Duchartre, Paris, 1931.

many languages. But the Portuguese chronicles and narratives of the period are in general unknown to the foreign reader.

The Portuguese Government has recently decided to publish in French an anthology of the Portuguese chronicles and narratives of Portuguese travellers of the fifteenth and sixteenth centuries.

Having been entrusted with this work, I have begun with the narratives of the Royal Chronicler, Gomes Eannes de Azurara, who relates *The Conquest of Ceuta* and the *Discovery of Guinea*. Azurara is the historian of the first overseas adventures of the Portuguese, the contemporary and the passionate admirer of the Infante Dom Henrique.

The Rise of the Aviz Dynasty

Dom Fernando, the last king of the Burgundian dynasty, died without offspring (1383).

Among the claimants to the crown was Dom João, his bastard half-brother, Grand Master of the order of Aviz, son of King Dom Pedro I.

Dom Fernando, a wise and intelligent administrator, had displeased the people by the scandal of his passion for Dona Leonor Telles, the wife of one of his vassals. He obtained the annulment of her marriage, and married her himself despite the opposition of his councillors and the people.

At his death a revolt broke out in Lisbon against the Queen and her favourite, the Spanish Conde Andeiro. Dom João, the bastard, set himself at the head of the movement. Andeiro was assassinated, and Dona Leonor Telles went to end her days in a Spanish convent.

The Cortes of Coimbra, in which the jurisconsult João das Regras defended the rights of the Master of Aviz, and the Battle of Aljubarrota (against the Spaniards), when the Constable Dom Nuno Alvares Pereira victoriously defended these same rights with the sword, gave the royal crown to Dom João.

The Master of Aviz ascended the throne. He married the English princess, Dona Felippa (Philippa), daughter of John of Gaunt, Duke of Lancaster; the mother of admirable princes, one of the most illustrious of whom was the Infante Dom Henrique.

With King Dom João I begins the dynasty of Aviz and the maritime epic.

The Infante Dom Henrique

The Infante Dom Henrique, Grand Master of the Order of Christ,[1] Duque de Vizeu, after the conquest of Ceuta, withdrew into the solitude of Sagres.

During this first expedition to Africa, on which he accompanied his father and brothers, he obtained information from the people of the conquered territory as to what they knew of that mysterious Africa which had attracted him as by a spell since his childhood; and his belief in a world beyond Cape Bojador was confirmed by the information which he had succeeded in gathering. Ceuta was then what Venice became a little later: the great commercial *entrepôt* of the East. And during the pillage of the city the Infante had

---

[1] The Templars were of great service to the first kings of Portugal in their conquest of Moorish territory, and they acquired much wealth and power in the new kingdom. After the suppression of the Order by Philippe le Bel, the Portuguese King Dom Diniz, in order to retain his powerful defenders, changed the name of the Order of the Temple within his dominions into that of the Order of Christ (1319).

seen in the bazaars and the wonderful palaces the treasures brought from India by caravans that crossed regions unknown to the people of Europe. The legend of Prester John, that undiscoverable Christian king, whose mythical kingdom was supposed to exist somewhere on the Dark Continent, was at this time generally believed; it fascinated the Infante and stimulated his desire. Dom Henrique would certainly have been acquainted with the narratives written at the close of the eleventh century by the Sherif Edrisi, treating of Spain and Africa, recounting strange voyages to the West, and speaking of *certain islands in which the sheep have flesh so bitter that it cannot be eaten, and where there are men with the heads of animals, and others whose hair is scanty and red, and most fair women.* And he must also have known the later descriptions of the Arabs Masudi and Ibn Said, who said that in the West the world came to an end *in vapours, mud, and the dread shadow of the Mare Tenebrosum.*

It was related that in 1331–1334 some vessels which had sailed westwards from Lisbon had found inhabited islands (the Canaries), and that in 1339 some Spanish sailors in the service of Henry of Castile had brought from these islands pelts and hides, wax, and captives.

Algarve is the southernmost province of Portugal. Divided from the rest of the country by lofty mountains, and from Spain by the Guadiana, nearly all its coast looks toward Africa. At the extremity of Cape St. Vincent, which stretches out like an arm in the direction of the Dark Continent, a tongue of land runs southwards; barely five hundred yards in width, and a thousand in length. It is covered with bristling rocks, and nothing grows there save some stunted junipers, lashed by the sea winds and the spray of tempests, and powdered with the sands of Africa when the simoon sweeps the desert.

This little rocky peninsula was known as the Sacred Promontory (*Sacrum*). Of old the Celts had built a temple there. St. Vincent,[1] the martyr, born at Saragossa and buried at Valencia, was removed from his tomb by the Christians at the time of the Arab invasion. According to the legend, the ship which carried his remains was wrecked off Cape St. Vincent (so named after this event), and the saint's body was washed ashore on the little peninsula, escorted and protected by ravens. A chapel was built there in honour of the saint, in which certain relics were deposited. For centuries the boats that passed before the twice sacred promontory saluted it by dipping their sails.

Sacrum became Sagres, which is to-day no more than a fishing village built amidst the ruins of the old town.

It was here that Dom Henrique installed himself on his return from the Battle of Ceuta; on this bare, rocky point of land which thrusts itself out into the waves, looking toward Africa, between the waters of the Mediterranean and those of the Mare Tenebrosum, "where the world ends." It was for this wild retreat that he left the brilliant Court of his father. He was then twenty-four years of age.

He was born at the point of intersection between the Middle Ages and the Renaissance. Mediaeval Catholicism had rudely fashioned his soul. But his

---

[1] The saint's body was removed to Lisbon in 1176 and interred in the cathedral which bears his name, and where it lies to-day, guarded by the tame ravens which are kept in the temple.

mind turned toward that scientific and rational mysticism which marked the period whose dawn was already rousing Europe.

This man, placed at the critical turning-point of Portuguese history, is like the steersman who, by a slow, powerful pressure on the tiller, changes the course of the vessel. Until then the destiny of the country was that of all nations in the first stage of individualization. The nation was not yet consolidated; the masonry of the foundations had not had time to harden.

And suddenly the Infante Dom Henrique comes upon the scene, the fierce incarnation of destiny. What does he want? He wants to know what lies beyond Cape Bojador; he wants to discover the road to the Indies by rending the veil of terror that hangs over the Mare Tenebrosum; he wants to win the empire of Morocco from the Infidels. And Portugal, like a youthful soul too soon leaving its frail body, leaves her untilled fields, her still depopulated territory, her unfinished buildings, and goes in search of another world.

A century and a half later Portugal had accomplished her destiny. The world had been discovered. But the dynasty of Aviz was exhausted; its last king— again a virgin prince of twenty-four, again a man bewitched by the secrecy of Africa—dragged the country into its last epic struggle; in the same African sands that saw the birth of the glory which carried the name of Portugal to the ends of the earth the heroic period of Portuguese history came by its end.

On the promontory of Sagres the Infante Dom

Henrique built a fortress, an observatory, churches, houses, and dockyards for the building of ships.

These ships were caravels, the wonderful Portuguese vessels which the famous Venetian navigator, Cà da Mosto (in the Infante's service), called *the best sailing ships that go upon the sea*, and of which the feluccas of the Tagus give us some idea to-day. Seventy-five feet in length, and 20 to 25 feet in beam, the caravels had three masts and triangular lateen sails, of which the pointed leach, reaching skywards, sought the wind. They were swift and handy, and it was their hardy prows that broke the way to the new worlds.

The Infante founded at Sagres a school of navigation, and gathered about him mathematicians and cosmographers, both Portuguese and foreign. The cartographer and maker of nautical instruments, Master Jayme de Mayorca, worked for him. Master Pedro, the specialist painter, coloured the charts and sprinkled them with symbolic signs which indicated the fauna and flora and particular features of the countries which were gradually being discovered. Pedro Nunes, the Portuguese mathematician and astronomer, and the royal cosmographer, wrote remarkable treatises on the art of navigation, and invented the nonius.[1]

Another son of the King, Dom Pedro, on returning from his long voyages, brought his brother Dom Henrique the book of Marco Polo, and some Venetian charts on which the southward contours of Africa were sketched in accordance with vague presumptions. This book and these charts encouraged the Infante in his hopes and desires.

[1] *Vide* the works of Joaquim Bensaude, French translation, Coimbra.

At Sagres he had for his companions not only scientists and specialists, but also nobles, knights, and squires who were nurtured in his household, under his own direction, and were devoted to him. It was to them that he confided the command of the caravels which year after year set out for the unknown, across that mysterious ocean which legend filled with phantoms and spectres.

The caravels sailed, one after the other. During the Infante's lifetime the islands of the Atlantic were discovered: Madeira, Porto-Santo, the Azores and Cape Verde Islands, and the whole of the African coast as far as Sierra Leone.

The impulse had been given; it never ceased to operate.

On all the African islands—until then unknown—all down the coast, from the Senegal to Cape Guardafui, on all the coasts and islands lying between the meridians of Suez and Tidor, and latitudes 20° South and 30° North, and on the Asiatic coast of Ormuz as far as Malacca, the Moluccas, Macao and Japan, the Portuguese established protected harbours, safe anchorages, citadels, and fortresses, acquired by contract or pacific alliances, or taken and retained by force.

". . . Always vigilant, they [the Portuguese] encircled or conquered and fortified the central and most important points of the tracks followed by the Arabs, Turks, and Italians, and above all the maritime routes and passages to the Gulfs of Arabia and India: Aden, Ormuz, and Malacca. Thus the old maritime and terrestial paths of transit for Oriental merchandise from Ormuz, by way of Bassorah,

Damascus (or Aleppo), and Beyrout, or from Aden, through Cairo and Alexandria, to Amalfi, Pisa, Genoa, Venice, and Ragusa, declined and were deserted. Thus the roots of the Osmanic power withered and died; thus the flourishing period of the Italian cities came to an abrupt end.

". . . In her triumphal maritime progress Portugal discovered the whole world; she shattered the mediaeval bonds that fettered the knowledge of mankind . . ."[1]

[1] WILHELM STORCK, *Samtliche Gedichte*, Paderborn, 1894. See also the works of Joaquim Bensaude (French translation).

VIRGINIA DE CASTRO E ALMEIDA

THE CONQUEST OF CEUTA

BEING

THE CHRONICLE OF THE KING DOM JOÃO I

CHAPTER I

How the Infantes persuaded King João their father to undertake the conquest of Ceuta

DOM JOÃO had said how greatly he desired that his sons should be knighted in a splendid fashion.[1] This he had said on many occasions, and without a doubt it was the thing that he had most at heart. He had before his eyes his three elder sons in the flower of youth, strong and comely and valiant; and he could not rest his eyes upon them without his desire was increased thereby; they must be knighted with all honours, and the greatest magnificence, for they were endowed by God with perfect bodies and all the noble virtues befitting princes of their rank.

And he said one day:

"When it shall please God to give this kingdom quiet by confirming the peace with Castile, I shall ordain royal feasts which will continue for a year. I will invite, from all the kingdoms of Christendom, all the noble lords and gentlemen who shall be of an age and a disposition for such diversions. And I shall ordain that during these feasts there shall be great tourneys and jousts, and great banquets, with the best fare that can be obtained in the kingdom and from foreign parts; and thereto dances and games of every fashion. And all these things will be in so great

---

[1] At this time (1412) Dom Duarte, the heir to the throne, was twenty-one years of age; the Infante Dom Pedro, twenty; the Infante Dom Henrique, eighteen. The other two sons were still children: Dom João, the future Constable, was only twelve, and Dom Fernando, the future martyr, barely nine.

abundance, and of such quality, that the people who will see them and enjoy them will never have known the like. And I shall give presents of such magnificence, above all to the strangers, that the greatness and pleasantness of these gifts will oblige these lords to speak of them with admiration to all their friends. And after all these things I will make my sons knights."

This was said by the King, and all those that heard him desired that these feasts should be held as soon as possible. But the Infantes, bethinking themselves of the nobility of their blood and the greatness of their lineage, did not by any means hold that their entrance into the order of chivalry should take place on an occasion of feasting. Nevertheless, they kept their own counsel until the peace with Castile was signed, saying to themselves that it might be that they would yet have chances of risking their life and showing in war of what they were capable; but so soon as the peace was concluded they understood that the opportunity of being knighted as they had intended to be was escaping them.

Being one day together, and the Count of Barcellos[1] with them, they spoke of this matter . . .

"Come," they said, "let us speak to the king our lord. We will ask him to devise some matter wherein we can prove ourselves and be knighted in a fashion

[1] The Count of Barcellos, a bastard son of Dom João, was born in 1377; he was thus fourteen years older than the heir to the throne, Dom Duarte. At the time of his birth no one could have foreseen that his father would be raised to the throne. At the age of twenty-five he was legitimized by his father. Ambitious and given to intrigue, he acquired great wealth and power. He was the first Duke of Bragança, and his line gave rise, a century and a half later, to the Braganza dynasty.

befitting the greatness of his state and the excellence
of our blood. The fashion in which the King has
thought to make us enter the order of chivalry is in
truth most unworthy of the greatness of such a
happening. It is not by feasts, even the most splendid,
that such a happening may be celebrated. Great
exploits, courage, deadly perils, and the spilling of
enemy blood, these are the things that open the path
of chivalry to such as we. It is for the sons of citizens
and merchants to celebrate the great events of their
life by feasts, for their honour cannot outstrip their
state, and their renown is in proportion to their
expenses."

This converse was still continuing when João
Affonso, Intendant of the King's finances, entered
the chamber . . . and as he was a man virtuous and
trusty, who enjoyed great authority in the kingdom
by reason of the confidence which the King reposed
in him, they apprised him of their intentions.

"Your thoughts," he said, "are great and noble,
and since you are of this way of thinking, I can tell
you somewhat that will enable you to accomplish
what you desire. Ceuta, which is upon the soil of
Africa, is a city of note and easy enough to take;
and this I know in especial from one of my servants
whom I sent thither to ransom some captives of
whom I had charge. He told me that Ceuta is a great
city, rich, and very goodly; it is encompassed by the
sea on all sides, excepting a small piece which joins
it to the land. In pursuance of your father's great
desire, and your own, I see nothing at this present
which could better afford you the occasion which you
are seeking than the taking of this city. It seems to

me, however, that you should speak of it to the King, and ask him to command that this thing shall be done, for this would be a thing befitting, and not these festivals, these banquets, this eating and drinking, in which there is only expenditure of victuals and waste of time, and whose memory soon fades without leaving any profit."

"Why," they said, "do not you yourself speak to him, telling him firstly all these things?"

"I have already spoken of them," said João Affonso, "and he did not respond as I should have wished, but rather treated the matter as a pleasantry. But so that the affair may take a better turn, do you go and find him, the four of you together, and speak to him of this matter, telling him such things on that head as may seem good to you. Perchance he will give you a better hearing than he gave me."

The Infantes immediately went, all four together, to find their father, and recounted to him all the converse which they had lately held . . .

But the King, whose mind could not readily be persuaded, fell a-laughing, inasmuch as he took their discourse for pleasantries, as he had done on hearing João Affonso . . .

The Infantes did not by any means feel defeated by the King's first reception of their thought. And having for a few days given their minds to a multitude of things, they met anew, and for the second time went to seek their father. To him they proffered the same request with such excellent reasons that the King no longer treated their plan as a pleasantry, but promised that he would reflect upon their proposal.

. . . The King sent for Master Brother João Xina

and Doctor Brother Vasco Pereira, who were his confessors, the Infante Dom Duarte, heir to the Crown, and other scholars of eminence who were in the city, and he convoked also some of his Council, though not many, and spoke to them under the seal of the greatest secrecy . . .

He wished to know if this conquest of Ceuta would be a service rendered to God. Some days afterwards he received from these councillors a reply in the affirmative. He assembled his sons, and said to them:

"You may hold, perchance, that I am delaying unduly in the matter of which you have spoken to me, and that here you may see a lack of desire on my part. On the contrary, however, although my age is far in advance of yours, I challenge you to have a firmer will than mine for the accomplishment of such an action. But because I have seen many other enterprises, and because I have had experience of their great difficulty, I know how hard they are to accomplish, a thing that is still hidden from your eyes.

"I told you the other day that before giving you any reply I wished to know if such an enterprise was a service rendered to God, for this question is the foundation upon which our labours should build. The second question is to know if we can accomplish it, for many things are good in themselves and desirable to men, but men have not the power to achieve them. I know already that this is truly a service rendered to God, and that from this point of view I ought to perform it. It remains to decide if I have the power to accomplish it; and in this regard I have had serious doubts, of which I will tender to you five, which need not of necessity occur together, but of which each one is enough to prevent the accomplishment of this project. And I will expound them to you, that you may consider what they are worth.

"Firstly, for the accomplishment of this exploit great expenditure will be necessary, and I have not the money, nor do I know where I can obtain it, for even if I were willing to obtain it of the people by levying taxes, I find that I should thereby suffer a twofold loss, the first being the scandal amongst the people, the second the betrayal of the secret.

"Secondly, I see that the city of Ceuta is so far removed from us that in order to fight it we should need not only the men of this kingdom, but also others from abroad, if they were willing to aid us; and all these men must be furnished with the necessary arms and equipment; and we should have need of artillery of different fashions, and of victuals in great abundance, for we do not know how long we should tarry before this city.

"And in order that all these things should be conveyed to this place, a very great fleet would be needful, of many great vessels—without counting the small vessels, of which I do not even speak—and there is no such fleet in my kingdom, and I do not see how I could obtain it.

"Thirdly . . . I have great doubts and very little assurance as regards the Kingdom of Castile; it may be that knowing me to be absent from my country the Castilians would essay to attack my domains, and it would be a very hard thing to remedy this later, for they would find the whole country without defence, and could do with it according to their will. To prevent such a thing I should have at least to leave some men on the frontier, and if I did this I should not have as many as would be needed elsewhere, for the city of Ceuta is very great and very strong, and in order to besiege it and fight it a great many men would be necessary, and not having these the enterprise would be a disgrace whereof the memory could not be effaced.

"Fourthly, even if God were to give me the victory, as I should like to believe He would, the taking of this city would bring me more loss than profit, for the Kingdom of Granada would be far more easily taken after our conquest of Ceuta. And tell me, what shall I profit if the Kingdom of Granada falls into the hands of Castile? On the contrary, I should only lose thereby, for I am very sure the Castilians hate us, and more than ever after the defeats which we have inflicted upon them. Hence the capture of Ceuta may very well result in the taking of Granada by the Castilians, which could not be pleasing to me, since the enlargement of their domains will render us weaker in the defence of our territories, and them stronger to avenge their late defeats.

"The fifth reason seems to me to have great weight, for wise men, before undertaking an exploit, should study it under all its aspects as profoundly as possible, and not only in its present effects, but in the future, considering not only the contrary events which may follow immediately, but also those which may ensue later.

"If God wishes to aid us in the taking of this city,

what renown or what honour shall we have of this conquest if, after taking it, we can neither maintain nor defend it? And on this point I have great doubts . . .

"On the other hand, the Moors who are in this city of Ceuta would engrave upon their hearts the memory of the wrong and the injury which our victory would have inflicted on them, and out of revenge they would fill their ships with the flower of their youth, and would come to attack our people in Algarve, who would be without defence in their manors, and they would deprive them of their life and their possessions. Above all, we should lose all hope that our merchants could send their merchandise upon any ship to the cities of the Mediterranean, which they now do so often; for the Moors would have the dockyards of their cities full of flatboats and ships, merely to prevent the passage of our vessels, and I need not tell you what would be the fate of those which they might take.

"See, then, what would be the advantages to us of so much expense, and so many efforts and anxieties, and how slight the hope of victory; for glory and honour would depend on our ability to retain the city, and I do not see how or by what means we could keep it and govern it.

"I am thus of the opinion that it would be far better to forget these projects than to attempt their execution, for this last reason is sufficient, without speaking of the other four, which are all as substantial, to prevent the accomplishment of our desire. However, if you perceive that these reasons are not just, tell me your arguments to the contrary; I shall acknowledge them in accordance with right and reason."

This discourse of the King's greatly afflicted the Infantes. Howbeit, having discussed among themselves what they had heard, they returned to their father with fresh arguments, refuting one by one, and with much wisdom, the contrary arguments of the King.

. . . There was no one in the chamber beside the King and his sons, but I write what passed (during all these interviews) with their approval, for it was the Infante Dom Pedro, later on, when he became Regent of the kingdom, who related to me a great part of these doings in order that I should write them in this chronicle.

Then all this was told me also by the Infante Dom Henrique, Duke of Vizeu, and lord of Covilha, in whose household I dwelt for some time by order of our lord the King; and this Infante, better than any other person in the kingdom, could inform me as to the very spirit of the principal things which constitute the true value of history; and this because, even as he issued from his mother's womb, he held, so to speak, against his heart the symbol of the Cross of our Lord Jesus Christ, for the love of Whom he had always a great desire to fight the Infidels, and in this desire he lived and continued all his life, as I shall relate to you in what follows.

And I make this declaration here, because I have noted that several chronicles, written by very capable authors, have given rise to serious doubts, merely for the lack of such declarations as that which I have just made.   . . .

The Infantes returned to the King some days later, setting forth their replies to all his arguments; but their father did not appear to be convinced by them. However, some little while later he sent for the Infante Dom Henrique, saying that since during their last interview he had heard him speak of Granada, he now wished to hear him in private, and know all that he had to say on the matter. And the Infante spoke as follows:

"It seems to me that all the things that we do in this world must be based in principle on three points: the past, the present, and the future. As for the past, I will refer to the time when God, by His grace, willed that you should be King; you had nothing more than a small portion of this city of Lisbon, for the castle was against you, and so were the strongholds of Almada, Cintra, Torres Vedras, Obidos, Santarem, and almost all the others in the kingdom; yet God chose to show you your path in such wise that without prejudice or loss on your part all these strongholds have come into your hands, and obey you and are subject to you. Therefore you should not now expect less of God; even if the Kingdom of Granada were to fall under the domination of Castile, there would still remain to you, with the aid of Heaven, power sufficient to thwart the designs of the Castilians if they should think to serve you ill or offend you. For it would be much easier for you to do so now than it was in the past, and this for many reasons which I need not recount to you, since you are perfectly well aware of them.

"As for the present, I see how that this exploit would be a service rendered to God, and I think on your faith and your Christian spirit; and reason tells

me that you ought not to refuse war against the
Infidels for fear lest it might be favourable to the
King of Castile; since even if he were our greatest
enemy he would be so only by accident (being a
Christian like ourselves), whereas the Infidels are our
enemies by nature.

"As for the future, I believe the capture of the city
of Ceuta cannot in any way cause a rupture of the
peace and amity which you have recently established
between us and the Kingdom of Castile, but very
much to the contrary, for the Castilians will perceive,
from the greatness of this exploit, the valour and
mettle of your subjects, and the marvellous force at
your disposal for the accomplishment of such a feat.
They will see also how that our taking of Ceuta will
facilitate the conquest of Granada. And even if all
these reasons were not enough to make them understand what I have just said, their ill-will could not
readily be manifested against us, for the conquest of
Granada is not an easy task, and when it is effected
they will have enough labour and care to keep and
maintain it. And, above all, our Lord God, Who is
the perfection of all things, seeing your goodwill and
good disposition, will be with you always, and you
will be able to say with the Prophet: Since the Lord
is my helper, I need not fear what men may do
unto me."

Thus the Infante Dom Henrique concluded his
reply, with which the King his father was well content,
and laughing, he clasped him in his arms and gave
him his blessing.

"Ah well, my son," he said, "I have no need of
other replies to reach a conclusion. This conclusion I

have already foreseen. I hold that no virtue can attain to perfection without exercise, as it is with all callings, each after its fashion, and above all that of the knight, since it calls for strength of body and of mind. Thus, if the *fidalgos*[1] and other valorous men of this kingdom do not find occasion to exert their strength, of necessity they will do one of two things: either they will seek quarrel among themselves and provoke such conflicts and disorders as we read that the Romans did when their wars were over, or they will do such injury to the men of Castile that peace may be broken thereby, which I would not have by any means. It seems to me, however, that even if the taking of Ceuta should bring us no profit, that very reason would suffice to make us receive as things useful the fatigue and expense that such an exploit will involve. As for the difficulty of detaining and holding Ceuta after conquering it, I leave this to the care of the Lord God. And even as He has power to make very great that which is very little, so He will be able, by His Divine grace, to give us the means to govern and retain this city.

"I therefore resolve, with the help of God, to begin this enterprise and continue it to the end. And since God has brought us here, and has willed that we should be together, you and I, at the moment of my taking this decision, it pleases me that you should be the messenger charged to bear this news to your brothers, and to inform them of my intention as I have now declared it to you."

It is very true that all the King's sons had a great desire to see this project adopted and accomplished;

[1] Men of noble blood.

but none of them desired it so strongly as the Infante Dom Henrique. For this desire was born with him, as I have said. Transported with happiness he knelt before his father, kissing his hands and assuring him of all his gratitude.

The Embassy to the Queen of Sicily. First preparations. The opinion of the Queen and the Constable concerning the plans for the conquest of Ceuta. The assembling of the Council

BEFORE all else it was necessary to obtain information concerning . . .

"the situation and the plan of this city, the thickness and height of its walls, and the nature of its towers and turrets, in order to know what artillery it would be necessary to employ . . . and also the anchorages that exist there, and what are the prevailing winds for ships at anchor there, and whether the beaches are open and sufficiently undefended to allow us to disembark without great risk, or whether the sea is so deep that one could fight directly from the ships." So said the King.

The King sent for two valiant and cunning men in whom he had all confidence, the Prior of the Hospital and Captain Affonso Furtado, and entrusted them with this difficult mission. Everything was to be done in the strictest secrecy, and this expedition was to be carried out without arousing the least suspicion as to the intentions of the King, whether at home or abroad.

The King said to his sons, concerning this cunning project:

". . . It is my desire to proceed by means of a very pretty dissimulation. It will be broadcast everywhere that I am sending these two ambassadors to the Queen of Sicily, who is a widow and wishes to re-marry, which I know by the request that she made of me, asking me if it would be pleasing to me that my son Dom Duarte should espouse her. Now, I shall presently send my reply, asking her to wed the Infante Dom Pedro, which I very well know she will not do; but this proceeding will be highly profitable, for the ambassadors will have occasion to pass the city of Ceuta, when they will be enabled to study and observe all that I need to know."

This plan was carried out as Dom João had conceived it.

. . . He at once had them supplied with money for the cost of their equipment, and he had two galleys got ready, the best in his dockyards, and ordered that they should be provided with all things necessary, as though they were going to make part of an armada; and this because, in addition to the splendour with which the ambassadors of such a king as himself ought to be surrounded, it was necessary also that they should be so armed and provided that they could defend themselves against any Moorish vessel which they might meet upon the way, and which might seek to attack them. The King also had very fine liveries made in the fashion and colours of his house for all those who were about to embark, and from the prow to the poop he had the galleys adorned with banners, canopies, and awnings of stuffs that were likewise of the colours of his house, which had never been seen aboard ship until this present; and the fashion has endured to our days, as you may see.

When all was ready, the ambassadors having taken

their leave of the King, the galleys put to sea. Having left Lisbon with all this luxury, they came before the city of Ceuta. There they cast anchor, making as though they would rest before pursuing the voyage. And the Prior, seated upon the deck of his galley, quietly and all at his leisure, like a wise man and a discreet, regarded and observed attentively the disposition of the city, taking account of all that he wished to know. And for his part the Captain right skilfully surveyed the beach, seeking for the spot where the rocks were fewest, that he might choose the place where the soldiers might be landed most readily; and so soon as night had fallen he left the galley with great caution, and in a small boat he passed all round the city, studying the anchorages and everything else that it befitted him to know. And on the morrow they were so well advised that they weighed anchor and continued their voyage . . .

The embassy to the Queen of Sicily met with no success, for she wished to wed the heir to the throne of Portugal and not an Infante. She accordingly rejected the King's proposals as the King had foreseen and desired.

When the ambassadors returned to Lisbon they were straightway received by the King, who was surrounded by his sons.

Captain Affonso Furtado was the first to be questioned by the King.

"Sire, I bring you but one reply: you have at Ceuta an excellent landing-place and a very good anchorage; you can go there in all security when you will; and the city, by the grace of God, will soon be in your power."

"Thus it will please God, I hope," said the King; "but I wish most of all that you should speak to me of the anchorage and other matters of which I charged you to take cognisance."

"I will say no more," said the Captain, "save that you can go thither, for all there is favourable and according to your desire; and I would add, Sire, that not only will you take this city, but many other fortresses, which, because you hold Ceuta, will fall into your hands and the hands of your descendants.

"And this, Sire, I know by reason of a marvellous event that happened when I was young, of which I have ever retained a faithful recollection, because of the extraordinary things that came to pass thereafter. And because it is now fitting that you should know it, I will tell you what befell.

"The King Dom Pedro your father, whose soul is with God, sent my father into foreign parts as ambassador; and as I was then very young, my father took me with him that I might see new countries and learn of divers things as we travelled. We came to an African port not far from Ceuta, where I did my best to see such things as seemed to me the most noteworthy. I passed a fountain which flowed into a fair watering-place, and I sat myself down close at hand, taking great pleasure in observing the beauty of the horses that were led to drink there, which were very numerous and all most worthy of admiration. An old man whose beard and gait spoke of advanced age drew nigh to me, and regarding me attentively asked me what was my country. I replied that I was Spanish.[1]—I should like to know, said he, in what

[1] The whole Iberian peninsula was then known as *Spain* or *the Spains*.

part of Spain you were born.—I replied that I was
born in the city of Lisbon.—And in what kingdom
does that city lie?—I replied that it was in the
Kingdom of Portugal.—And what king rules this
kingdom at present?—A very good king, I said, who
is called Dom Pedro, the son of the excellent King
Dom Affonso who fought in the Battle of Salado.[1]
Dom Pedro is a just king who greatly loves his people.
—Tell me, if you please, said the old man, how many
sons has this king.—I replied that he had three: the
first Dom Fernando, the second Dom João, and the
third Dom Diniz.—Has he no others? asked the Moor.
—He insisted, begging me to search my memory well,
but I did not bethink me of you, Sire, for you were
then very young . . . and suddenly I remembered
your birth, and I said: Friend, it is very true that
the King has yet another son, very young, who is
called Dom João, but I did not remember him because
among us bastard sons are not held in such honour
as lawful sons.—Yes, he said, it was for that reason
that I wished to know.—And with a great sigh he
bowed his head and wept, at which I was greatly
astonished; and as his tears continued, and his
affliction was very great, I besought him to tell me
the reason of a grief so profound. He refused for a
long time to do so, but in the end, overcome by my
insistence, he said: Friend, my tears are but trifles
compared with the cause that makes me weep. And
do not believe that I am weeping for anything that
pertains to the present; my pain is born of my know-

[1] A famous battle which the allied Kings of Castile and Portugal
fought against the Moors, who were defeated with enormous losses
(1340).

ledge of the misfortunes that will befall my fellow-countrymen and my friends. And since destiny has led you to this place, give ear to what I shall tell you. This king, Dom Pedro, who is now your sovereign, will not live long; and on his death his eldest son, Dom Fernando, will reign. He will wed a wife who, after the death of Dom Fernando, will be the cause of great rebellions, and the two other sons of Dom Pedro, through the fault of their sister-in-law, will go to Castile and will there end their days. This youngest son of the King, whom you see to-day despised in comparison with his brothers, will be as the spark from which a great conflagration springs; for a day will come when he will first of all avenge the dishonour of his brother, and will then be chosen by the people to ascend the throne. He will have great quarrels with the Kingdom of Castile, from which he will always emerge victorious; and he will be the first King of Spain to have possessions in Africa; and it is through him that the destruction of the Moors will begin. And he, or those who will be born of him, will come to this fountain to water their horses.

"See now, Sire," continued the Captain Affonso Furtado, "I who heard these things, and who saw thereafter how all things befell in the same order in which this man foretold them, I cannot doubt that the city of Ceuta will fall into your hands. And for this reason I repeat what I have already said: that you will have all things according to your desire—the landing-place, the anchorage, and all."

The King was a man who set little value on such things: he began to laugh, making a jest of the words of Affonso Furtado; and he told him thereupon that

D

he had entrusted him with this mission only that he might obtain precise information as to what he knew, for he held the Captain to be a man capable of obtaining good information in respect of these matters. . . . But all these reasons could not get a word more out of the Captain, who would not tell the King more than he had already said.

Dom João then spoke to the Prior, commanding him to say what he had learned concerning the situation of the city of Ceuta, and all the other matters with which he had been charged.

"Sire," said the Prior, "of all that I have seen I will not say a word until you have had brought hither four things: two sacks of sand, a roll of ribbon, a half-bushel of beans, and a basin."

"Do you not think, then," said the King, "that we have had enough of follies with the Captain and his prophecies?" And he laughed most heartily; but then he commanded the Prior to have done with jesting and to declare what he had seen.

"Sire," said the Prior, "it is not my habit to jest with your lordship, but I repeat that I will say nothing until I have these things that I have desired of you."

The King's brow began to darken, for he believed that his ambassadors had failed in the charge that was laid upon them.

"See," he said to his sons, "what wise replies are given me by men of such authority! I ask them for news concerning the matter of their mission, and the one speaks to me of astrology, while the other speaks of things that savour of sorcery! Who would have believed that such men would have acted in such a fashion?"

The Infantes, being well aware of the worth and intelligence of the Prior, could by no means believe that he had returned from his voyage without bringing the desired information; they assured him of their confidence in him, and besought him to reply to their father.

The Prior laughed to himself, for he saw that the King had by no means divined his intention; but he repeated that with all goodwill he could not reply unless he was given what he had asked. The King then had the things brought, and the Prior shut himself up with them in a chamber. Then, with the sand, he reproduced the hill of Almina, with the whole of the city of Ceuta, as it stands, with its hills and valleys; and Aljezira with the mountains of Ximeira, exactly as they are situated. When this labour was completed he called the King and the Infantes, and said to them:

"Now you may see the result of my observations and you may ask me all the questions you will, and I shall answer you with my experience before your eyes."

The King considered this reproduction for a long while, and the Prior expounded everything to him, telling him the thickness of the walls on the seaward side and how the towers were placed, and what was their height; then he showed the King the fortress with all its defences, and which were the places that ought to be attacked, and all the other matters which the King desired to know . . . and the King was well content, and gave great praise to the Prior for his excellent description. He concluded from this that the situation and defences of the city were sufficiently favourable to the enterprise which he was meditating.

Some days after the Prior's demonstration the King declared to his sons:

"I have given much thought to our enterprise, and it seems to me that there will be two difficult obstacles which must be overcome before we can begin. The first is the Queen, my dear and well-beloved spouse, who, by her high virtues and her great goodness, is so loved by all that if she does not give her consent to our projects neither the people nor the great men of the kingdom will help us with the vigour and activity of which we have need. The second obstacle is the Constable, who, as you know, by his holy life and his high exploits, has so bound all the folk of this kingdom to him in gratitude and devotion that if he is opposed to our plans all will consider that they are bad and will give us only unwilling aid."

Listening to their father, the Infantes were plainly anxious, for they believed that neither the Queen nor the Constable would approve of their designs. They went to find their mother, and unfolded to her their great desire, and entreated her to give them her support in approaching the King. The Queen received them most kindly; straightway she asked for an interview with her husband, to whom she spoke as follows:

"Sire," said the Queen, "I am going to make you a request which is not such as a mother commonly makes in respect of her children, for in general the mother asks of the father that he will keep their sons from following any dangerous courses, fearing always the harm that might befall them.

"As for me, I ask you to keep them from sports and pleasures and to expose them to perils and fatigues. The Infantes came to see me to-day, and recounted to me your conversations regarding those plans concerning the city of Ceuta of which your Intendant of finances, João Affonso, had spoken to you. They added that your disposition toward this subject was not so favourable as they could have wished, and they besought me to intercede with you in favour of their desire and mine.

"For myself, Sire, considering the line from which they are descended, a line of very great and excellent emperors and kings and other princes, whose name and renown are broadcast in the whole world, I would not by any means—since God has pleased to make them perfect in body and mind—that they should lack opportunities of accomplishing, by their fatigues, their valour, and their skill, the like high feats as were accomplished by their ancestors. I have therefore accepted the mission with which they have charged me, and their request gives me great joy. I am of opinion that their desire is good and does honour to their youth, and I beseech you then so to order all things that they may exercise their strength and their virtues as they should; and it seems to me that you have a good opportunity of doing so now, by realizing what you have already discussed with them; and for my part I shall be under a great obligation to you."

The noble manner in which the Queen supported them gave the Infantes great happiness, and the King, well content to see the obstacle which he feared thus disappear, began immediately to make preparations for his enterprise.

. . . The first thing which he undertook was the

victualling of his dockyards, and he further made inquiry as to how many vessels there were and in what repair; also he immediately caused trees to be felled for the building of the galleys and flatboats that were lacking to make up the number of those which he wished to take, namely fifteen galleys and fifteen flatboats, and he engaged the carpenters and caulkers for the building of the said vessels and the fashioning of all that pertained to them.

The King also commanded that all the copper and all the silver to be found in the kingdom should be collected, and he sent for as much more from abroad, signing contracts with the merchants on the best terms that he could obtain, so that in a very short time he had a great abundance of these metals. João Affonso, Intendant of the finances, was bidden to furnish all the revenues of the city, and to make arrangements with the Treasurer of the Mint (without telling him a word of the secret) and cause him to make ready all the furnaces, which were very soon working; and so the work of coining money began, and continued actively day and night. Mice Carlos, the Admiral, was given warning, by order of the King, that he must make provision for all the mariners, each according to his rank, so that they were equipped and ready to do swiftly whatsoever the King should command them to do.

The Secretary of State was ordered to obtain information of the number and age of the men who would be liable to be called up for service in the army.

All these preparations began to perplex and disquiet the people, and each essayed to divine their purpose. Yet this was but the beginning of an activity which increased continually.

However, the Infantes waxed impatient. Eighteen months had passed since they had first spoken to their father of this enterprise of Ceuta. The preparations must be pressed on; greater haste must be made.

Nothing had as yet been said to the Constable, Dom Nuno Alvares Pereira. After a lifetime of splendid exploits he was living in retirement on his estates, and a halo of sanctity was forming about his venerable and powerful personality.

A public interview with the King would give rise to speculation, and the secret of all these preparations must be kept. Accordingly a hunting expedition was organized, which lasted for several days. As though by chance, the King on the one hand, the Infantes on the other, gradually drew near to the domains of the Constable. And thus the interview took place without giving the people cause to think that a conference of the greatest importance was being held.

And when they were together the King recounted all that had passed, and the preparations which he had begun to make; adding, however, that he had no intention of undertaking anything until he had heard the opinion of the Constable.

"My opinion," replied the Constable, "is that this plan was not conceived by you, nor by any other person of this world; but that it has been revealed by God . . ."

The second obstacle (the opposition which the King had feared to encounter from Dom Nuno Alvares Pereira) had therefore ceased to exist.

When the Infantes returned to Santarem, where the Court was at this time, they reminded their father that they would ere long have been waiting for three years. And the King replied that he would assemble his Council in the month of June, and that then he would expound his plans, and the date of their departure would be fixed.

When the time had come for assembling the Council the Infante Dom Henrique went to the King and said:

"Sire, before all these matters are more advanced, and because I see now that they will be brought to a successful conclusion, I am going to beg you to grant me two favours:

"The first: that I may be one of the foremost to disembark when, if God so wills it, we arrive before the city of Ceuta; the second: that when your royal ladder is set against the wall of this city I may be the first to ascend it."

The King beheld him with a smile, and answered him:

"My son, may God bless you as I bless you for your goodwill to serve me and increase the honour of your name. For the moment I will not reply to any of these matters, but if God permits I will do so at a time and place more fitting."

The King repaired to the city of Torres Vedras, where the Count of Barcellos, the Constable, the Grand Masters of the Orders of Christ, and Santiago, and Aviz, with the Prior of the Hospital, and many other lords who were members of the Council, were already forgathered.

The King was uneasy. He was full of apprehension concerning the attitude of the councillors when he should lay before them the project of the taking of Ceuta.

The Constable said to him:

". . . It seems to me that you ought not to present

this feat as a new thing but as a matter already decided upon by you as just and good, for your chiefest aim is to serve God well . . . and if you speak of this to the Council it is by no means that they may say whether or not it is good, but to have their opinion as to the best means of bringing this enterprise to a successful conclusion. And in order that this may produce a good effect you will command that I shall be the first to speak, and I will so contrive that none of them, after they have heard me, can oppose our plans."

All passed in the Council as the Constable had foretold. After the King had discoursed the Constable spoke, giving high praise to the plan for taking Ceuta, and exalting the holiness of this enterprise; and in conclusion he offered his aid and his services to Dom João. Then the heir to the crown, Dom Duarte, spoke, and the Infantes.

None of the lords, after such professions of faith, dared to oppose the least argument to what had been said.

And when João Gomes da Silva, famed for his strength and his valour no less than for his wit and his joyous humour, cried: "As for me, Sire, I have only this to say: On with you, greybeards!" all burst out laughing.

Greybeards! Excepting the Infantes, all those who were present had silvery hair. They had taken part in the Revolution; they had given the throne to Dom João; they were the victors of Aljubarrota and a thousand battles against the Castilians; but their hearts were still young, and their adventurous enterprise against the Infidels tempted them, recalling the days of their youth, of their warlike ardour, filling them with the old joy and enthusiasm. The "greybeards" took to their hearts the dream of the Infantes.

CHAPTER III

*Of the challenge which was sent to the Duke of Holland,
and of other Embassies, and of all the preparations for
the enterprise against Ceuta which had been ordered by
the King*

THE King convoked the Council anew. It was
needful to discuss what would be the best means
of keeping secret the aim of the preparations for war,
and the equipment of the fleet, which must be put in
hand at once. It was necessary to invent some pretext
which would divert the attention of the public in a
direction opposed to that of the actual goal, lest the
Moors of Ceuta should take alarm.

It was decided that they should challenge the Duke
of Holland, threatening him with war if he would not
set his face against the injuries and thefts of which
his subjects were guilty in respect of those Portuguese
merchants who had to traverse his states.

. . . And to this end it was decided forthwith that
Fernão Fogaça, Intendant of the Infante Dom Duarte,
should travel in the quality of ambassador in charge
of the mission. And at the same time the date of
departure when the fleet would sail on the enterprise
of Ceuta was fixed at one year from that time, about
St. John's Day of the following year. Fernão Fogaça,
having received his letters of credit and the King's
orders, proceeded to Holland. So soon as he had
arrived he made it known to the Duke that he had
been sent to him on behalf of the King Dom João
of Portugal, and that he asked for the favour of an

audience. The Duke replied that for the moment the ambassador must wait; and that he would inform him of the date when he would be received.

Fernão Fogaça, so soon as he had returned to his lodging, sent to the Duke very secretly that he wished to speak to him alone, because this conversation was the true purpose of his embassy; and that what would be said afterwards in public was only a means of concealing this mission.

The Duke therefore received Fernão Fogaça unknown to any, and the latter told him of the projects of the King Dom João, and how it was needful that he should have a pretext for the warlike preparations which he was making in his country, in order that the Moors should not be alarmed. And that the King of Portugal begged him to accept this challenge as though it were a true challenge, and that for this he would be most grateful, and would prove his gratitude at the first opportunity.

The Duke replied that he thanked the King Dom João heartily for confiding to him so great a secret, and assured the Ambassador that he would take good care to keep it. And as for the challenge, he would reply to it in such a manner that all the world would believe in the reality of this feint.

Some days later the Ambassador of the Portuguese King was received by the Duke with great pomp, with all his councillors. Fernão Fogaço set forth his mission and uttered a threat of war if the Duke did not take the needful measures to prevent the thefts which the Portuguese merchants suffered in his states. The Duke appeared to be highly indignant at this threat, and replied that he had no fear of such a war, even if all the Spains were to attack him. And his councillors had difficulty in appeasing him. He dismissed the Ambassador harshly enough; but when the night had fallen he sent for him secretly, and entrusting him with the most affectionate greetings to the King his master, the Duke took leave of him very graciously.

So soon as Fernão Fogaça had departed the Duke made it known throughout his states that the King of Portugal had sent him a challenge, and that all must be prepared for the possibility of war.

In the meantime Dom João hastened the preparations for the expedition to Ceuta. He sent certain squires to all parts of the coast of Galicia and Biscay, and into England and Germany, to charter as many tall ships as could be obtained there. Very soon the news had spread in all directions that the King of Portugal was making ready for an enterprise of great moment.

When Fernão Fogaça returned with the Duke's reply the King was well content with it, and he at once had the news spread abroad throughout the country that the chief captains of the great fleet would be the Infantes Dom Pedro and Dom Henrique. He never declared that the war would be a war against Holland, but sometimes he let it be understood, and sometimes he spoke in a veiled manner of greater projects; so that no one knew exactly what was on foot.

The King confided to the Infante Dom Henrique the task of assembling all the men-at-arms of the north country and having them put on board at Porto; and to the Count of Barcellos he entrusted the same task in respect of the centre; and all the south country he entrusted to the Infante Dom Pedro, who was to have his men put on board at Lisbon. The heir to the throne, Dom Duarte, was entrusted with the finances of the kingdom, and with justice.

Thus the King distributed among his sons the tasks of preparing for the war, and of administration. He himself took charge of the armaments and artillery, and all things relating to the fleet.

. . . The Infante Dom Duarte, when this charge was confided to him, was only twenty-two years of age. These two charges are by their nature so important, and the Infante was so young, and so little accustomed as yet to such responsibilities, that he entered upon his labours with the greatest concern. He rose so early to go to Mass that the rising sun found him already in the law court, where he remained until the eleventh hour and the twelfth. And when he had barely finished eating he proceeded to give audience; and without allowing himself a moment's rest he returned to the work of expediting the course of justice and the business of the kingdom's finances. In this manner but little time was left to him for sleeping at night, and this fatigue engendered a malady of melancholy humours which increased with the continuance of these labours. And as he was so gentle and courteous by nature that he could never give anyone an ill reply, and as on the other hand the character of this malady is to give the sufferers a distaste for their fellows and a longing for solitude, there was a great battle in the soul of this good prince. For by nature he was given to seeking out people and hearing their requests with attention and kindness, and his melancholy sickness made all such matters tedious to him. But his virtue and his kindness were so great that they had always the better of the frowardness of his malady, so that there were very few who even suspected that he was suffering . . .

. . .

Who in these days could speak of anything but arms and munitions of war? The King had written to all the lords, *fidalgos*, and men of substance, apprising

them that for his service and for the honour of the
realm he had resolved to send his sons, the Infantes
Dom Pedro and Dom Henrique, as captains of his
fleet, to serve him in all that he might command
them to perform, and that it would be pleasing to
him if all these lords were with the Infantes in this
undertaking; to which end he commanded them to
hold themselves in readiness, to make their preparations, and to declare to him how many men each of
them reckoned to bring, in order that he might at
once send them the money needful for their equipment and that of their men, and for their pay.

This news set all the realm agog, and everywhere
men were busied only in cleaning and preparing
arms, making biscuits, salting meat and other victuals,
fitting out the men-of-war, and arming the ships. . . .
This business was at its height in the cities of Lisbon
and Porto especially, and there was no one in these
cities who was not thus occupied.

In Lisbon this work was performed with such ardour
that on a still day the sound of it was plainly heard
in several villages of the Ribatejo. In sooth it was a
sight most fair to see, how all this bank of the river
was full of caravels and vessels of every sort, around
which day and night the caulkers and other artisans
were swarming like ants; and, on the other hand, one
might see multitudes of bullocks and cows beheaded,
and many men busied in flaying them, while others
cut up the meat and salted it, and packed it in barrels
and hogsheads.

The fishermen and their wives had no other thought
than to gut and salt whiting, dogfish, skate, and other
fish, and whenever the sun shone with its full heat

nothing could be seen but the fish spread out to dry.

The great hammers of the mint were never still night or day, and the press of work there was such that a man shouting among the furnaces could not be understood.

The coopers had not a moment's rest, continually making or repairing barrels and hogsheads for the wine, meat, and other victuals.

The tailors and weavers never ceased their weaving, cutting, and sewing, making liveries of divers fashions and colours in accordance with the orders of the lords. The carpenters were at work the livelong day, making chests, and packing the bombards and cannon, and all the ammunition for the artillery, which was heavy and numerous. And the ropemakers made without resting cables and top-ropes and many other ropes of hemp for the ships, as well for those of the kingdom as for those which came from foreign parts . . .   . . .

Amidst all this manual activity men's minds were likewise at work, seeking to divine the goal of the expedition and the true projects of the King. Opinions were many and various; some saying that the King was sending his daughter, the Infanta Izabel, to England, there to espouse a prince of that country, and that all these troops and the fleet were going thither to help the King of England to conquer France; or that their object was to go to the Holy Land and bring back the Holy Sepulchre; or to make war upon the Duke of Holland; or to fight and overthrow the Pope of Avignon; and other suppositions beside, one more absurd than another.

. . . Howbeit, no one gave, nor even suspected,

the true reason of all these preparations. Only a Jew, a servant of the Queen Dona Felippa, who was called Juda Negro, and who was a good troubadour, sent to Martin Affonso of Athouguia, who was squire to the Infante Dom Pedro, some verses which recounted the marvels of the Court; these rhymes repeated all the suppositions which I have related, and many more beside; and in the last quatrain he added that the wisest folk surmised that the King's intention was to attack the city of Ceuta. But he did not say this because he had heard speech of it; he said it because he was very wise in astrology and made great use of this science . . .

This uncertainty as to the true intentions of the King Dom João was felt not only in Portugal but also abroad. The Government of Castile was uneasy. The peace had been sworn in Castile but not in Portugal. Ambassadors came to Lisbon and were astonished by the courtesy and affection which the King Dom João showed them, for they had feared lest the warlike preparations of this sovereign should have as their object a new war against their country.

So likewise the King of Aragon sent ambassadors to the King of Portugal, for he wished to know whether the latter had the intention of attacking his states. But he was reassured by Dom João's reply.

About this time foreign lords who had heard of Dom João's great preparations for war came to Portugal to offer him their services. Among them were a puissant baron of Almain and three great seigneurs of France;[1] and all gave good proofs of

---

[1] The names of the French noblemen have evidently been mutilated by the chronicler. He calls them Mosem Arredentão, Pierre de Louvre Batalha, and Gibotalher.

their valour. These lords were magnificently equipped and were surrounded by noble squires of their country. The German baron had forty such squires.

The Moors of Granada, perceiving that the King Dom João was giving all manner of warranties to the kingdoms of Castile and Aragon, and accepting the services of German and French lords (of which they were well informed by the Moorish freemen living in Portugal and trading there), began to fear lest this war should be unloosed upon them. Accordingly the King of Granada also sent his ambassadors to Lisbon.

These told the King Dom João that neither the Moors of Portugal nor those of Granada dared any longer trade their merchandise between the two kingdoms, since in view of the great preparations for war they feared to lose their wares; and in the name of the King of Granada they besought the King of Portugal of his goodness to give them guarantees.

"I know not," replied Dom João, "what reasons the Moors may have for harbouring such suspicions when they have no knowledge of my plans . . . and I do not see any reason why I should give you the guarantees for which you ask me. Say then to your king that I have no intention of undertaking against him or against anyone what he fears (in respect of merchandise), since I have never in my life done such a thing. And this is the end of what I have to say to you, and you may return when you please."

The Moors understood that this reply did not give them any guarantee, and they then spoke to the Queen, in the hope of obtaining from that quarter a better result. . . . They told her that Rica Forma, the chief wife of the King of Granada, begged the Queen Dona Felippa to concern herself with the

E

mission with which the Moorish ambassadors were charged. Rica Forma knew well, they said, that the prayers of women had much power over the hearts of husbands when they asked their spouses for things on which their hearts were set; therefore she besought the Queen, out of regard for her, to be pleased to persuade the King to give a favourable reply . . . and that since the Queen Dona Felippa had a daughter to marry, she might very soon receive thanks for her good offices in this affair, for Rica Forma assured her that she would send her for her daughter the finest and richest outfit that any Moorish or Christian princess in the world had ever possessed.

But who could have persuaded the Queen to follow such a course? For the Queen was a woman most acceptable to God, and would never espouse the interests of the Infidels, nor do anything in their favour, the more so as she was English, and England is one of those nations that hate the Infidels.

"I do not know," she replied, "what may be the manners of your kings with their wives. Among Christians it is not the custom for a queen or princess to meddle with the affairs of her husband in such cases, since for this they have their councillors, and their wives are the wiser the more they hold themselves aloof from matters which do not concern them, and avoid knowing what they cannot understand; for their husbands, with their councillors about them, have all the cares of the matters with which they busy themselves with that devotion which the honour of their condition imposes upon them. It is very true that queens are not by any means kept so far removed from everything that they cannot at times make a request of their husbands touching those things which they desire; but these requests must be of such a nature that they could not be refused; and those princesses who do not act thus are not deemed wise and discreet. And you will also say to your queen that I thank her for her goodwill, but that as to the outfit of which you speak, she must do as she pleases, for, with God's grace, my daughter will have all that she needs for her marriage. And make your request of the King, my lord; for if it is good he will grant it with a good heart."

Seeing that their approach to the Queen had not benefited them, they sought to obtain by large promises the support of the Infante Dom Duarte . . . "and because the King of Granada, our lord, desires to obtain the guarantees and securities which we are asking, he begs you to take our request to heart, since he knows that the King your father will allow himself to be guided by your counsel . . . and that you may not hold your pains fruitless, the King of Granada vows to give you in exchange such a present as all the nations of the earth will think magnificent, and of this you shall have at once any guarantee you demand."

"Those of my country who are in high places," replied the Prince, "have not the habit of selling their goodwill for a sum of money, for if they did so they would deserve to be called merchants and not lords or princes. Therefore your promises are useless; for if your king were to promise me, not a present of money, but his whole realm, I would not accept it, for I could never ask of my father anything but what is just and reasonable. But the King of Granada, your lord, has no cause for fear and need not be disquieted."

And so the Moorish ambassadors returned into their own country, and they were not well content with the answers which they had received.

CHAPTER IV

*How the Fleet was organized, and of the enthusiasm of
all for the mysterious enterprise. How the Queen Dona
Felippa sickened of the Pest, and of how she died*

IT beseems me that it is now time to set these
matters on one side and to speak of those things
that have to do with the organization of the fleet;
howbeit, before this I shall tell of the goodwill which
all men had to serve the King in this enterprise.
Each did his part with as much joy as if he were
fully certain of winning a glorious victory without
facing any danger; and the ignorance of the true
purpose of all these preparations did in no wise lessen
the enthusiasm of these people.

The men of the realm were divided, so to say, into
two parts: those who had ever served the King, and
who were all much of an age; and the sons of these,
who ardently desired to acquire the merits of those
who had given them life, and following their example,
to furnish proofs of courage and loyalty. Like the
offspring of greyhounds, who inherit from their
parents the natural faculty of the hunter, so in general
the sons of valiant men have in them the desire to
acquire the merits which ennobled their fathers . . .

. . .

So all went well, and in all the realm there was
such a stir of work that ere long the preparations
were all but complete. Nothing could hold up these
men, nothing check the ardour of the Infantes, and
above all of the Infante Dom Henrique, whose fleet

at Porto,[1] so well provided and equipped, was the admiration of all, for he was very young, and had not yet much experience; howbeit he acted with the knowledge and wisdom of an old captain inured to this fashion of work. Nothing checked them, not even the pest which broke out in divers parts of the realm; it was said that it had come in some of the vessels brought from foreign parts, from countries in which it was raging.

Men were busied not only with the things needful for the fleet, the army, and war, but also with those which might contribute to the splendour of such an enterprise. Dom Henrique did not forget to have magnificent liveries made for all his captains; and these lords in their turn clad their men in the colours of their houses.

The desire to take part in this mysterious expedition was so great in all men's minds that it gave rise to the most unexpected results.

. . .

. . . Ayres Gonçalves de Figueiredo, a noble knight of ninety years, sought out the Infante Dom Henrique, accompanied by his squires and his men-at-arms, clad in his coat of mail, bearing himself upright, and not having the appearance of a man of his age. And when the Infante saw him draw near to kiss his hand he began to laugh, and said to him:

"It seems to me that a man having lived such a great tale of years is deserving of rest after so many battles and fatigues."

"I know not," replied Ayres de Figueiredo, "if my limbs have grown weak by reason of age; but the will is as firm to-day as ever it was in all the battles which I fought in your father's service. And I deem

---

[1] Porto, O Porto, "the port"; Oporto.

there could be for me no greater honour at the hour of my death than to be one of you in this enterprise."

And two squires of Bayonne who had rendered the King great service during the war, and had received great benefits thereby, and who were not much younger than Ayres de Figueiredo, sought out the Infante and asked him to give them provision for the expedition.

"All that you have done hitherto in your lives," said the Infante, "is full enough, and I am obliged to you for your goodwill. It beseems me, however, that you ought not to go, for at your age a man has the right to rest."

But the squires would by no means hear of resting, and the rather showed themselves wounded by this reply.

"What shall I do?" said the Infante; "all the arms I had are already given out, and I have no more to give you."

"A valiant man," they said, "never sells his arms, even in times of the greatest difficulty. As for us, albeit on certain occasions our pay has not reached us, our weapons have never left us. Give us then victuals, and do not trouble yourself in the matter of arms."

The Infante was well pleased by this reply, and gave them presents over and above their pay; for such goodwill on the part of men so aged was a thing well deserving of reward.

I know not if I speak as a pagan, but in sooth I do believe that in these days the very dead wished that their bones were clad with flesh, that they might rise from their tombs and accompany their sons and their kinsmen on this undertaking; and I will say, moreover,

that if the living demeaned themselves thus joyously,
the souls of those who, being now in divine splendour,
knew all the truth rejoiced in it even more.

In testimony of what I have said above you must
know what befell a monk of the order of St. Dominic,
who was in the city of Porto on the second Day of
the Litanies: as he had been enjoined to preach that
day during the procession he rose incontinently after
the first crow of the cock, and, reciting his prayers on
his knees before the altar of the Virgin Mary ere he
entered into his oratory, marvellous visions appeared
to him: among the which he seemed to see the King
Dom João before the Virgin Mary, armed at all
points, on his knees, his hands being folded and lifted
toward the heavens, whence was presented to him a
sword, whose brilliance could not be likened to any
earthly thing; but the good monk could not see who
held the sword, for his eyes could not endure this
divine splendour. And this monk, being a simple man,
would relate this vision to none but another monk,
his friend, who was the sacristan of the monastery.

Ah! how loath were the souls of the brave men who
were dying of the pest to part from their bodies! It
was not so much the natural regret which seizes upon
all souls on quitting the flesh, but above all regret
that they must depart from this world without seeing
the end of this enterprise!

. . .

When the Infante Dom Henrique had completed
his preparations he had a sloop made ready in which
he sent his squire Affonso Annes . . . to warn the
King that the Infante, his son, was leaving the city
of Porto with his fleet. And immediately the Infante

gave the order to all that they should embark for the departure. The ordering of this fleet was glorious; all the ships of war, galleys, and other vessels were adorned with the great standards of the chevaliers of Christ and little flags with the colours and the device of the Infante; and as they were new and richly adorned with gold, men marvelled to behold them.

Tilts and canopies of rich stuffs in the colours of the Infante, and bearing his written device, covered the decks of the galleys; and the captains were the lord Infante and the Count his brother . . .

. . . and there were seven galleys and seven captains, and these, no less than all those of the other ships, of no matter what condition, bore the livery of the Infante, which was of two sorts: in silken twill and in fine woollen cloth; and, to the contrary of what one might have believed, the persons of high rank wore the liveries of woollen, and those of lower rank the silken garments.

Since we have spoken of the captains of the galleys you must know likewise who were the chief officers of the other fleet: Dom Pedro de Castro, son of Dom Alvaro Pires de Castro, Gil Vaz da Cunha . . .

. . . All these men bore the livery of the Infante, as well as the other *fidalgos* and squires whose names we do not know in particular; and when the day of departure had come very great was the joy that prevailed among all these men of the fleet, for in all the ships there were trumpets and other instruments whose sound uplifted their hearts . . .

. . . And there was thereto yet another cause of contentment, which was that on this day they all had new garments; and this, by the novelty of the thing, still further increased the joy in the hearts of all whomsoever, and above all in the hearts of the young men—and he who has little experience of the same has no need of further proof. And over and above the livery which the Infante thus gave to all these lords and *fidalgos*, and in general to all his followers, each of them gave his livery to his servitors; but it would take us too long to describe the colours and the device of each one of these, and we will do no more than declare those of the Infante, which were garlands of holm oak overlaid with silver, surrounding the device *Power to do well*; and the colours were white, black, and blue . . .

. . .

. . . So soon as the King was aware of the news which told of the near arrival of the Infante Dom Henrique at Lisbon he required the Infante Dom Pedro to go forth and encounter his brother. The eight galleys of this other fleet were speedily got to sea, as well as all the other ships. In the first galley Dom Pedro was embarked, and in the second the Grand Master of the Order of Christ . . .

. . . The Constable, and all the lords besides who accompanied Dom Pedro, took their places in the ships' boats and other small craft; and if the Porto fleet was well bedecked and adorned, this was in no wise less splendid; and they differed but in the devices, for this fleet showed everywhere only the device of the King. The Infante Dom Henrique had so disposed his fleet that the smaller ships were the first to cross the bar of the Tagus; then the great ships, and last of all the galleys; and of these the last was that of the Infante. And all these ships filling their sails advanced upon the city, preserving their formation about the Infante's galley, and this formation was such as to make them appear even more in numbers than they were. And at last the two fleets met together, reuniting the two brothers, who had great joy thereof, since there was not between living men amity greater than theirs.

The Infantes Dom Pedro and Dom Henrique were two of those five sons of the King, the like of whom never was so obedient to their father and bound together by so great affection. There is no writing which could make us believe that ever the like was seen.

And these two princes, companied by their fleet, ascended the river as far as that place where the Infante Dom Henrique in after days caused a church to be built which is called Santa Maria de Belem . . .

. . .

And now you must know that when the Infantes came to this port of Restello, as I have told, they brought their ships to anchor there while the other ships sailed up the river with great sounding of trumpets and other instruments, as though seeking to declare the joy of their hearts to those who were on shore . . . and Affonso Annes, that squire of the Infante who had carried to the King the news of his arrival, came to tell his lord that the Queen, his mother, was sick . . .

. . . The Queen lay sick of the pest. She had caused three swords to be fashioned, of which the scabbards and the guards were adorned with gold and pearls and cut stones; and it was with these swords that she wished her sons to be knighted by their father.

"Sire," she said to the King, "I require you as a great favour . . . to have the kindness to knight your sons before me, at the moment of your departure, with the swords that I shall give them to this end and with my blessing. It is said that arms offered by women weaken the hearts of chevaliers; but I believe that, having regard to the line from which I am descended, the swords which the Infantes receive from my hand will by no means enfeeble their hearts."

Howbeit, she was stricken by the pest; and her state rapidly worsened. The physicians no longer had hope of saving her, and she herself knew that her death was at hand.

Until the last moment she encouraged the King and the Infantes, speaking to them of their enterprise and the need of departing so soon as might be.

. . .

. . . and immediately they brought her the swords the Queen summoned her sons to her side; taking the greatest of the swords, she said to the Infante Dom Duarte: "My son, God has chosen you among your brothers that you may be their heir to this kingdom and that you may hold in your hands its government and its justice. Knowing your virtue and your kindness I give you this sword of justice, with which you will govern great and small when at the death of your father this realm shall be yours. I commend its people to you and pray you ever to defend it with all the steadfastness of your soul, never suffering that any do it wrong and being watchful always that right and justice be served. And note well, my son, that whereas I say justice I mean justice with compassion, for justice without mercy is no longer to be called justice but cruelty. I wish that you might be dubbed knight with this sword, for I have caused it to be made, and with it the other two, that I might give them to you, and that you might all three be made knights before me by your father before your departure; but God has willed otherwise.

"Howbeit, I require you to accept this sword from my hand with my blessing and that of your forefathers from whom I am descended . . ."

The Infante Dom Duarte, with great respect, knelt and kissed the hand of the Queen, saying that he would obey all her commands, and it is very sure that he never forgot the words of his mother, and that he was faithful to her commandments until the hour of his death.

The Queen was right glad to hear his answer, and lifting her hand she gave him her blessing. She then called to her side the Infante Dom Pedro, and said to him:

"My son, since your childhood I have ever seen how greatly you are concerned respecting the honour and service of ladies and damozels, which is one of the things that are especially to be commended to knights. I have reminded your brother of his devoirs to the people; and for you, I recommend you to have always in mind the care of defending and protecting the honour and happiness of ladies and damozels."

He answered that he would obey her with all goodwill, and kneeling before her and kissing her hand he received the sword and his mother's blessing.

You shall consider what must have been the Infantes' fullness of heart as they heard their mother's words. With all their might they held back the tears which without this would have flowed in abundance; but their countenances were profoundly sad as they listened to the words of the Queen, so full of love and wisdom, and the calm knowledge of death so close at hand.

But we have still to relate what befell in respect of the third sword. The Queen summoned the Infante Dom Henrique:

"My son, come to my side." And the countenance of the Queen lit up with joy (for he was yet all but a child), and her lips smiled gaily:

"You have seen the gift that I have made of the other swords which I have given to your brothers. This third sword I have kept for you, for as you are strong, so it also is strong. I have charged one of your brothers to protect the people; and the other, women. To you I wish to command all the seigneurs, chevaliers, *fidalgos*, and squires of this realm, for albeit they all belong to the King, and he is careful of all according to their condition, yet they will often have need of your aid in order to maintain their rights and receive the benefits and rewards which they may deserve; for often, by reason of the false witness and abusive requests of the people, the kings take action against them, which thing they should never do. And thus I have chosen you, knowing the love you have ever shown them, that you may take them under your protection, not only through the inclination of your heart, but also in duty. I give you this sword with my blessing, and I desire that with it you shall be dubbed knight."

I cannot declare in writing the great sadness which

weighed upon the Infante Dom Henrique as he listened to his mother . . .

"Lady," he said, "be very sure that so long as my life endures I will cherish the memory of what you have just commanded me; and in order to obey you I will employ all my power and all my goodwill."

And he kissed her hand, saying how greatly he thanked her for the sword which she had given him, whose value was for him beyond reckoning.

The Queen, having heard these words, strove to smile, and lifting her hand blessed him . . .

. . .

After this converse of the dying Queen and her sons a very great wind began to blow. The Queen asked what wind this might be, and the Infantes replied that it was the north wind.

"I believe," she said, "it is a good wind for your voyage." And the Infantes replied that it was the best.

"How strange a thing is this," she said. "I looked with so great joy for the day of your departure, thinking of the pleasure of seeing you knighted; and lo, I am become a hindrance to this departure, and I shall not behold the thing I so desired."

The Infante Dom Duarte sought to hearten her, saying that he had seen sick persons much nearer to death recover their health; and that she would yet see them knights.

But she answered him:

"Yes, I shall see you from on high; and my sickness will not prevent your departure, for you will set forth on the day of St. Iago."

All were astonished to hear this, for this feast would take place in a week. Yet her prediction was realized.

And a little after this the Holy Virgin appeared to her. The Queen lifted her face toward the heavens, all transfigured, and said:

"Praise be to you, Holy Virgin, since it has pleased you thus to come from Heaven to visit me." And drawing the sheet of the bed against her bosom she kissed it and fell into contemplation.

Seeing this, the Infantes sought to draw the King away, for they understood that their mother's last moment had come. But he did not wish to leave her, and he did so only upon the decision of his councillors, who begged him to depart, lest the sight of his dear wife dead should rob him of the courage to pursue his enterprise.

As the heat was excessive, the Queen was buried during the night, and as secretly as might be. And on the morrow, in the morning, her obsequies were held with very great magnificence.

The Infantes clad themselves in drugget, as also did all the great folk of the realm; then they went to the village of Santa Maria de Belem on the bank of the river near the fleet. And there they assembled the Council, and it was decided that the departure for Ceuta should be made as soon as possible.

Certain councillors having doubted that the fleet could set sail so promptly after these days of uncertainty, the King asked of the Infante Dom Henrique:

"Would our fleet truly have need of longer preparation in order to put itself in readiness for departure?"

"Sire," said the Infante, "you may embark forthwith and give the order to sail when you will, for the only preparation needful will be to weigh the anchors and hoist the sails."

"Since this is so," said the King, "we shall depart

on Wednesday . . . and do you, my sons, return to the fleet and make all things ready, so that we sail, with the aid of God, on Wednesday. And, since in feats of arms there should be neither sadness, nor tears, nor mourning, but that wholly to the contrary, the chevaliers should be accoutred in their finest garments, in order that this may rejoice their hearts, put off your drugget and array yourselves as before your mother's death, and even better if may be, and let all the other lords do likewise. Later, if God is willing, we shall choose another moment for our mourning."

The Infantes repaired immediately to the fleet, and the Infante Dom Henrique invited his brothers to dine with him on his galley. When they came on board Dom Henrique changed his apparel, and their fine clothes were taken to the other Infantes; and all the galley was adorned, and the order was given to the trumpeters to place themselves in the highest part of the ship and sound the most joyous airs.

It was a Sunday, and the men in the other vessels of the fleet were at play or resting, for by reason of the ravages of the pest they shunned setting foot ashore. They were greatly astonished to hear the trumpets . . . and the captains caused their ships' boats to be launched and were rowed to the Infante's galley . . . and so soon as they knew the reason of all this joy, and that the fleet would leave in three days' time, they returned to their ships in great haste and caused them to be adorned with flags.

The fleet was a thing most wondrous to behold; in the morning it was like to a forest which had lost all its leaves and fruits, and lo! of a sudden it was

F

changed into a magnificent orchard, resplendent with
green leaves and flowers of varied colours; for the
standards and the flags were innumerable and of
diverse shapes and colours. And one might have said
that in this orchard strange birds had suddenly begun
to sing, for in each ship diverse and numerous instruments were playing without respite, and the music
did not cease to make itself heard all that day . . .

. . .

The news quickly reached the city, and there
excited all manner of commentaries and contrary
opinions. For the people, who had greatly loved the
Queen, did not understand how the King could have
permitted such rejoicings immediately after the death
of his spouse. Some accused the King of allowing
himself to be persuaded by his sons, above all by the
Infante Dom Henrique, to undertake this mysterious
enterprise at a moment when the body of the Queen
was hardly cold.

Speaking of the Infante Dom Henrique, people
murmured:

"The King has always held this son as being more
of a man than the others in feats of arms and combats
. . . but killing wild boars in the forests of Beira is
one thing, and slaying armed men who are able to
defend themselves another. Do they think perchance
that this is a matter of jousts and tourneys in which
no one will dare to unhorse the Infantes? May it
please God that all this does not come to an ill end,
for there are many things in this affair which give
rise to doubt."[1]

[1] Before sailing for Ceuta, Dom João appointed Dom Fernando
Rodrigues de Sequeira, Grand Master of the Order of Aviz, who had
succeeded the King in this dignity when the latter ascended the throne,
to be Regent of the realm during his absence.

CHAPTER V

Of the voyage and the arrival of the Fleet before Ceuta.
Preparations for battle: dreams and celestial signs

THE piety of the King Dom João was always very great . . . and it was said that on the day of departure, having on board an altar well adorned, so soon as the sails were unfurled he fell to his knees, and lifting his hands and his eyes to the heavens he prayed as thus:

"Lord, since by Thine infinite grace, among all the marvellous things which Thou hast vouchsafed to me, Thy insignificant servant, Thou hast given me kingdoms and territories over which I reign, and the strength to vanquish mine enemies, I pray Thee, of Thy divine mercy, to remember in this moment me, and this people which belongs to Thee, and which Thou hast confided to me, and all of us who are here ready to dedicate ourselves to Thee. Accord us the victory over the enemies of Thy holy faith, and reserve for another time the expiation of our sins.

"And you, Senhora, the Holy Virgin, who have always been the advocate of my actions, continue, I pray You, to grant me Your aid, so that by Your merits I may have the victory over that of which You know, the victory which I ask of You so earnestly."

The cold wind began to swell the sails, and pushing them across the bar of the river carried the fleet out to sea. This was a thing so lovely to behold that those who saw it could not conceive of a pleasure greater than this . . .

In all the high places of the city of Lisbon the people gathered in great multitudes, and followed with their eyes, as it were in a ravishment, the departure of the fleet.

"Oh, Lord!" said these people, "Thou has manifested a very great love for the people of Portugal in giving it such a king to govern it! Happy the day that beheld his birth, for he has set the true crown upon the head of His people!"

And they said: "May good fortune lead and guide thee! May the fame of thy victory be such that all the princes of this world are jealous of thee!"

. . .

Thus the whole fleet held on its course, and on Saturday, about the close of day, it rounded the Cape of Saint Vincent. By reason of certain relics which were there, all the ships saluted the cape with their sails, in token of veneration; and that night they cast anchor in the Bay of Lagos. On the Sunday the King disembarked and assembled his Council, and it was decided that the moment had come to declare plainly to the people the whole truth regarding the purpose of the enterprise. The order was thus given to Fra João de Xira to preach before the people and tell them the King's intention in undertaking this great expedition . . .

Fra João de Xira preached the sermon and declared the whole truth to the people; and addressing those of the fleet, he enjoined them to repent of their sins and to take the firm resolve that they would not relapse into their faults. He read to them the Bull of the Pope, by which the Holy Father granted absolution to all those who should die in fighting the Infidels on this crusade . . .

. . .

The Moors of Gibraltar were greatly disquieted when they saw the Portuguese fleet arrive before their city. In their alarm they found no other expedient than to send the King Dom João the best and most precious things they could find, while asking him to assure them of peace. But the Portuguese King would promise them nothing, and confined himself to accepting their presents.

At Tarifa the King of Castile had as Alcade one Porto Carreiro, who was Portuguese by birth. When the fleet had come to the entrance of the Straits the people of this city were amazed, for they had never beheld such a multitude of ships. But as presently all the vessels lowered their sails, and as this happened at the fall of night, they told themselves that assuredly this vision had no reality.

. . .

They said one to the other:

"Surely they were phantoms."

But a Portuguese who was among them said:

"I believe rather it is a manifestation of the power of the King of Portugal, my lord, and nothing else."

"If all the trees of Portugal had been cut into planks," said the others, "and all the Portuguese turned into carpenters, they could not in the course of their lives have built such a multitude of ships."

"You will see ere long," said the Portuguese, "what they are that you now call phantoms; you will perceive that they are real ships full of brave men and well armed, and flying the Portuguese colours. They will pass before your eyes."

But they would not believe him . . .

. . . And on the morrow it so happened that the morning was misty, and nothing could be seen upon the sea. The sound of trumpets and other instruments was heard; and these people of Algesiras believed that they were listening to a celestial music. Suddenly the sun shone brightly on the vast fleet, which was passing slowly before the walls of the city. Who was the man in that city who could refrain from casting everything aside to come and gaze at such a marvel?

"I am very sure now," said the Alcade Porto Carreiro, "that this is the work of the King Dom João. When I think on the exploits of this man it seems to me that I dream, like Jacob. Bethink yourselves," he said again to those who stood about him; "you have never seen nor heard speak of any king of the Spains or of any other country whatsoever who has assembled a fleet as numerous."

. . .

And immediately when the ships had cast anchor before Algesiras he caused to be prepared a great offering of cattle and sheep, which he bade his own son, Pedro Fernandes, to present, with his homage, to Dom João. The King was well content with this, and said that he accepted this proof of the goodwill of the Alcade and his son with great pleasure. But as for the cattle, he begged that they would keep them, for his ships were well provisioned and he had no need of them.

. . .

So soon as Pedro Fernandes came ashore again he sprang upon a horse which he had left there, and began to gallop, frightening and wounding with stabs of his lance the bestial collected by him on the shore. Which those of the fleet beholding, they straightway killed all these cows and sheep, and took what profit they might of them. Then the King and all the lords who were there present gave high praise to the son of the Alcade and thanked him for this deed.

But this same Pedro Fernandes thereafter performed another deed for which the King was even yet more thankful to him. This gentleman having heard that a great Almogavare of the Kingdom of Granada was in this neighbourhood, attacking and robbing the young people who went inland in search of fruit, he undertook to punish him. And having perceived him in the very moment when he was carrying off one of these boys, he seized him and imprisoned him in an old hut near which there was a tower, where he caused him to be hanged.

But the Moor was greatly honoured in the matter of this justice which was done upon him, for many persons, and of very high rank, came readily to see him, and immediately he was hanged they assailed him and larded him with blows of their swords. Pedro Fernandes did this in spite of the peace which then existed between the Kingdom of Castile and that of Granada. In exchange for this good service rendered to the Portuguese he received his reward, for the King sent him word that immediately he returned into his kingdom he would expect a visit from him. And Pedro Fernandes did not fail to accept this invitation; on this occasion the King had delivered to him a goblet filled with a thousand golden *dobras*, so that with this money he might buy a fine horse. He received also many jewels, which were worth as much more; and the Infantes made him presents of great value, which gave him great happiness.

The King, being before Algesiras, there assembled his Council, and resolved to attack the city of Ceuta on the following Monday. He therefore undertook the voyage on that day; but there came up a great fog, which hindered the fleet from sailing directly to Ceuta. The currents being in this place very powerful, the whole fleet was carried toward Malaga, saving only the ship of Estevam Soares de Mello, and some of the galleys and flatboats and smaller craft, which arrived before the city that very day. A great disquietude seized upon the Moors. Howbeit, they beholding only a few vessels, and not the whole fleet, and having no assurance what might be the intentions of the King Dom João towards them, they were not for the moment alarmed beyond measure, contenting themselves with closing the gates of the city and climbing upon the walls the better to behold the fleet, rather than thinking to defend themselves.

. . .

In the end, however, the Moors became uneasy, above all Salabensala and certain of the wise elders of the city; and they sent their orders to all the parts round about that the men should hasten thither weaponed and provided, as a measure of precaution.

Then those who were upon the walls of the city began to fire cannon and arbalests upon the fleet, the which was proof how completely they had already lost all hope of peace. But the missiles did not reach the ships, which were out of range, saving only the Admiral's galley, for that lay nearer. Nevertheless the Admiral would not move away, saying that since fortune had placed his ship in this position he would remain there and abide the danger, for they had come thither to advance and not to retreat.

Certain young Moors came down upon the beach to fight against the Christians, and these incontinently hurried thither in their ships' boats and fought for a long time. Several Moors met their death in these skirmishes, and in the end the others took refuge in the city.

The Wednesday following the King decided to anchor with the ships that accompanied him on the other side of the city, and there await the rest of the fleet. And seeing that this did not come up, he sent Dom Henrique on his galley in quest of the Infante Dom Pedro, with orders to cause all the other vessels to come as swiftly as might be and join him at this point.

Dom Henrique found his brother sorely tormented, for the pest, having been brought from Lisbon, had declared itself upon several of the ships, and the men were downcast and disheartened by this plague, and by the fog and the currents which had borne them away from the other ships.

However, the orders were given, and all the ships made for Ceuta to rejoin the King.

The two Infantes sailing together on the same galley, it befell on the Friday morning that a fish rose out of the sea, and lifting itself in the air came and fell upon the deck of the galley; and they ate of it that day. . . .

. . . and I who write this history have never seen nor yet heard tell of such a thing; to me it seemeth marvellous, and, according to my thinking, far removed from natural things . . .

All this time the agitation of the Moors of Ceuta was constantly increasing. Some weeks before this they had seen signs in the heavens; a star had appeared near the moon, greater and more brilliant . . . "than any other star of the thousand and twenty-two which the astrologers had numbered, whose altitude can be measured" . . . and other strange and unwonted signs. A Moor who was a holy man, during the time of Ramadan, had a dream which troubled him: he saw clouds of bees above the city of Ceuta, and a lion, bearing upon his head a golden crown, entered the strait in company with a multitude of sparrows, which flew upon the bees and exterminated them. Many astrologers were summoned by Salabensala to study the signification of these signs and this dream. After the council which they held the most famous of all of them said:

". . . in the days of the great Miramolim, when, for the first time, he landed on the soil of Spain, there was a Moor who was digging his garden hard by this city. So digging he destroyed some ancient foundations, pulling away the stones, and he found a piece of marble on which was graven the image of our prophet Brafome, a native of Morocco, whose feet were resting on an inscription in four lines, which said thus: From the house of Spain will come forth a lion with three lion cubs, his sons, in company with a great fleet laden with many men, and he will oppress the noble city. Alas! his might will lead to the destruction of these regions of Africa. Moors, seek your safety in flight! Do not wait until he brandishes his sword!—This prophecy accords with the dream of this Moor, seeing that he says that he beheld a lion crowned with gold entering by the strait. We are the bees, and the sparrows represent the Christians. When Cordova was torn from us a Moor of that city had the same vision in a dream" . . .

. . .

The Moors were sorely distracted on hearing the opinion of the astrologers, but that befell which must always befall when fatality must follow its course.

While the fleet, baffled by the fog, the currents, and a great tempest, which threatened to destroy it, was stayed from assembling before Ceuta and making ready for the battle, the Moors would have had time to make preparations for defence. But they hesitated, irresolute, not knowing what course to follow, and they were taken by surprise as though they had not perceived the manœuvres of their enemy.

Amidst all the difficulties they had to overcome— contrary winds, fog, tempests—the King's councillors gathered round him and debated the manner of assailing the city so soon as the circumstances would permit.

At length one day the King Dom João said to the Infante Dom Henrique:

"My son, I am mindful of the request which you made of me when we were yet in Lisbon: I told you then that I would reply to you when the time had come. And now the time has come. You asked of me permission to be among those who should be the first to leap ashore for the attack. I grant you this, but it does not please me that you should be among the throng, but rather as chief captain." And in speaking thus all the King's countenance was shining with joy, which told of the great hope that he placed in the strength and ability of his son.

"As for us," said the King, "this day, about night-fall, we shall anchor our fleet before the city; and you will go with your fleet toward Almina, and there you will anchor, and we shall be on the other side, in such wise that the Moors, beholding in this place the better part of the fleet, will believe that the attack will be opened here. Thus they will bring their forces here to hinder us from landing, while they will guard less strongly the side that is toward Almina. And you, so soon as you see my signal, will cast your planks ashore and will disembark as swiftly as you may. When you are masters of the beach we shall bring our fleet alongside of yours, and we shall follow you in such sort that you will not be long alone.

"I recommend you further," said the King, "so that the currents may not carry your boats toward Malaga, as they have already done twice, to place your galleys in such a manner that even if the current should carry away some of the boats, they cannot be carried too far."

. . .

. . . So soon as the Moors of the city beheld the fleet quite close to its walls they set lighted lamps in all the windows to make the Christians believe in a multitude of defenders who did not exist, for the men summoned from the surrounding parts, having seen the fleet depart, had gone their ways. And since the city was great, and was illumined in this sort on every side, it presented a very goodly spectacle . . .

. . .

Even as the Moors lit their city with innumerable lights, so the men of the fleet lit their vessels; and this was much rather of necessity than to give the false seeming of a strength greater than that of which they could dispose. For so soon as the ships were anchored each man busied himself in making all things in readiness for the morrow; and with the torches that the captains had carried before them, and the lanterns that the men had at hand to light themselves at their labour, all the fleet was resplendent, and the lights seen from the city appeared to be even greater in number than they were, for they were multiplied by their reflections in the water, and the whole fleet seemed afire, which caused great astonishment among the Moors. But when the night was more advanced, and the lords withdrew to their cabins to sleep, one by one all the lights went out . . .

   · · ·

The sun was not late in beginning his day's labours, for this fell on a Wednesday, the twenty-first day of the month of August . . .

. . . The men of the fleet who had passed the first part of the night in working on deck were still sleeping. When they beheld the sun darting his rays upon the sides of the ships they began to call one another by whistling, or shouting the names of their friends; and they set to work, furbishing their weapons, and scanning them closely to make sure that nothing was wanting; others hastened, with tools under their arms and hammers in their hands, to rivet their armour; others tested the leather points of their doublets; others, recalling their sins, sought the priests, laying bare to God the great repentance which was in their hearts; others tried their battle-axes, swinging them with all their might, so to discover if anything might hinder them in their movements; others drew their swords from their scabbards, brandishing them, and making sure that they were sharply whetted.

"Ah," they said, "my good sword! How well you have cut, when it has pleased God, despite the iron of plate-armour and coats of mail! We shall see to-day what you can do in the way of hacking the flesh of these dogs who cannot bear the weight of plate-armour!"

Others opened the kegs which contained their best provisions, and offered these to their friends, saying:

"Let us eat, for it may be that this is the last day of our life; and if, by the grace of God, we are still living after the victory, we shall then have enough of victuals."

On their side the Moors displayed great activity in the labour of preparing their defence. They could be seen running from this side and that upon the walls, testifying thus that fear was very far from their hearts . . .

CHAPTER VI

How the City of Ceuta was taken by the Portuguese

WE must say somewhat of the feelings of Salaben-sala when he realized the intentions of the King. Salabensala was a man of advanced age; he was descended from the noble line of the Seafarers, the best of all those in Africa; and he was the lord of the city of Ceuta and of many other cities on the shores of this sea. You may imagine what must have been his thoughts when he beheld these new neighbours who had suddenly arrived before the gates of his city.

As the wisest men are those who perceive with the clearest sight such things as are great and perilous, Salabensala was well aware of the power of the King Dom João. Although the exploits of this prince had been accomplished on the other side of the sea, Salabensala was by no means ignorant of them. He knew how Dom João had accepted battle against the King of Castile, although the Portuguese forces were but few as compared with the great and splendid army of the Castilian sovereign; and how the King of Portugal had vanquished and completely routed the Castilian; and how thereafter he had for so long a time sustained against the same enemies great and numerous battles, from which he had always issued victorious. Thereto Salabensala told himself how great must be the wisdom of Dom João, that he should have contrived thus to bring so great a fleet against Ceuta without that any, even to the last moment, had knowledge of it.

"How may I prepare the city against an attack so formidable, and arrange for the defence in so short a time?" Salabensala asked himself. ". . . How warn the King of Fez? Before he has time to assemble his army the walls of Ceuta will be levelled . . ."

Being thus deep in these thoughts, a throng of young Moors came to him . . .

"It is not so great a thing to see the Christians thus come upon us," they said. "Their numbers are not so many that we cannot oppose them. Who knows? it may be they will give us the occasion for a great victory . . . it may be that all this beauty of their fleet will after all remain in our dockyards; that all their gold and silver plate will serve for the wedding-feasts of our children; that the rich adornments of their chapels will bedeck our mosques in token of our victory.

"Their fleet," they said, "is divided into two parts, and we believe that they will disembark to-day. We will go to encounter them on the beach, and there we will make a great carnage, for the greater number and the best among them are covered with iron, and for this reason their movements must be slow and difficult; whereas we are light and swift, and shall be able to attack them with great advantage. Once fallen to the ground, it will be hard for them to rise again. How can they rise when they are as heavy as rocks? . . ."

And as the Infante Dom Henrique was awaiting only the signal of his father in order to disembark, Martin Paes, who was his chaplain, took in his hands the consecrated Host, and showing it to all the

Christians assembled before him he spoke to them thus :

"Brothers and friends, it has seemed to me that no man can have a good issue of the thing he undertakes if he does not know for what end he is undertaking it. And it is very possible that you do not exactly know why you are here. Know then that you have come to render service to Our Lord Jesus Christ, Whom I present to you at this very moment, and for the love of Whom the King our lord has undertaken this expedition . . ."

The words of the chaplain Martin Paes strengthened the hearts of all who were in that ship. But as in the other vessels no other priest spoke to the men, and as the sun was already waxing hot, they became impatient in that they had not received the order to attack, but were still awaiting the signal, which was long in coming. The Moors ran down on the beach and defied the men of the fleet, thereby increasing their desire to go ashore and give battle.

Then João Fogaça, who was squire to the Count of Barcellos, being no longer able to endure such delaying, went down into his boat and commanded the rowers to take him to the shore. The first man to leap ashore was one of his companions, Ruy Gonçalves, he who afterwards became commander of Canha and squire to the Infanta, the wife of the Infante Dom João. But the Moors did not find it so easy to throw him down as they had told Salabensala, for immediately he was on the land he began to smite them with such blows that they had to withdraw from this place where the boats were to land.

The Infante Dom Henrique leapt into a boat,

G

taking with him Estevam Soares de Mello and Mem Rodrigues de Refuios who was his lieutenant, and he commanded the trumpets to sound the attack. When the Infante leapt ashore the number of those from the fleet was beginning to increase upon the beach. Ruy Gonçalves, who had been the first to arrive, was already fighting at a distance, beside a German gentleman, and they had overthrown a Moor of very great stature, who was distinguished among the rest by his strength and valour.

· · ·

. . . the Christians already disembarked on the beach were nearly one hundred and fifty, and they attacked the Moors hotly, wounding many and causing them to draw back, pushing them towards the Almina gate. The first to pass through this gate, fighting and encompassed by Moors, and to find himself in the city, was Vasques Annes Côrte Real, and immediately after him the Infante Dom Duarte, and behind him the rest; all struggling with fury in a great mellay with the Moors.

Then the Infante Dom Henrique recognized his brother; although the Infante Dom Duarte had already for some time been in the thickest of the fight, you must not believe that men in such circumstances, and armed at every point, can readily recognize each other. But when Dom Henrique knew his brother he made him a grand salute, saying that he rendered thanks to the Lord God for giving him so good a companion.

"And to you, Lord," he said; "I thank you a thousand times for your goodwill in coming thus to our aid."

The occasion was not fitting for the exchange of

many words, for the lances and stones were not idle.
And the battle continued, the Christians still driving
the Moors toward the gate of the city and wounding
and killing them without pity . . . and among all
these Moors there was one, very tall and of a most
threatening complexion, all naked, who used no other
weapons than stones, but each of the stones that he
threw seemed to be hurled by a catapult or a cannon,
such was the strength of his arm. And when the
Moors were thrust back as I have said against the
gate of the city, he turned back to the Christians,
stooped himself, and threw a stone which struck
Vasco Martins d'Albergaria and carried away the
vizor of his casque.

The aspect of this Moor was such as to inspire
terror, since all his body was black as a crow, and
he had very long and white teeth, and his lips, which
were fleshy, were turned back. But Vasco Martins,
despite the violence of the blow received, did not lose
countenance and did not fail to pay the Moor for his
labour; he had had barely time to turn round when
the lance of the Portuguese pierced him through. So
soon as the Moor fell lifeless all the others were taken
with panic and rushed towards the gate to take refuge
in the city, and the Christians with them . . .

. . . Vasco Martins was the first to enter the city
. . . and the first royal flag that floated in the city
was that of the Infante Dom Henrique . . . and
when the Infantes entered they were followed by
five hundred Christians . . .

The Infantes, the Count of Barcellos, and those
who were with them, finding themselves in the city,
took up their position on a sort of little hill which

had been gradually formed by the accumulation of ordures from the houses, which these people had long been casting away in that place. There they held their own, waiting until the other Christians from without should come to their aid. The five hundred of whom we have spoken would by no means be enough to disperse themselves and continue the battle at different points, for the city is very large, and there would be danger in so doing, since the Moors might have closed the gates, preventing the others from entering in their turn. But the time of waiting was not long, for the men of the fleet made haste to disembark, and very soon they came in a throng. And Vasco Fernandes d'Athaye did not wish to enter by the gate which the Infantes had already passed. He therefore went aside from those who were going in that direction, and in company with some of his uncle's foot-soldiers he proceeded along the wall on the outer side, until he had come to another gate, which he straightway began to batter down. Other Portuguese then coming up, and giving themselves likewise to this work, with blows of the axe and with fire they succeeded in destroying these gates. But this was not done without great difficulty, and seven or eight Portuguese, less well armed than the rest, found their death there, for their enemies were many on the wall, and their strength was constantly increasing, and they defended the gate by casting before the Christians, from the height of the walls, stones and weapons . . .

Vasco Fernandes with his men destroyed the gate, but he paid with his life.

. . .

There were already very many men on shore, so that the Infante Dom Henrique, at his brother's request, commanded that the men should be divided into troops, each of which would advance independently . . .

. . . and the Infante Dom Duarte said that it would be well if his brother and he were to go along the containing wall in order to take possession of all the high places before the Moors had time to take refuge there. And the sun being already very hot and the hill hard to climb, the Infante Dom Duarte put off divers pieces of his armour, for it was heavy to carry, and the Moors were already beginning to depart from the city. The Infante Dom Henrique could not follow his brother, for he still wore his armour, and Dom Duarte had to stop twice in order to wait for him; then he too put off the greater part of his armour, keeping only his coat of mail . . . he ran to rejoin his brother . . . and after some time they had to separate, each going his own way, and the Infante Dom Duarte took in succession divers high places, and the highest of all, which was called Cesto. And do not believe that these points could be captured without difficulty, for the city was still full of Moors, and one could not go a few steps without discovering numbers of them. But the Infante Dom Duarte never found enough of them to satisfy his desire. . . . Many things might be related of his courage and his exploits; things which if told of another man, however brave, would be considered heroic; but the Infante did not wish that anyone should speak of them, for they were all far below what he could have wished . . .

The King, who had remained with the Infante
Dom Pedro and part of the fleet on the other side of
the city, was waiting to give the signal of the attack
when the Moors assembled on that shore. He did not
know that the others had already disembarked and
that the battle was joined. Fearing, however, the
dangers of longer delay, he sent the Infante Dom
Pedro, attended by one of his squires, to the Infante
Dom Duarte with the order to disembark.

The reply was soon received. The King knew then
that the attack had begun, and that the Infantes
Dom Duarte and Dom Henrique were already, with
their men, in the city. Straightway he caused the
signal to be sounded, so that all those who were on
board this portion of the fleet should be landed and
should join the others.

The captains and the lords, having heard the news,
were by no means content, but murmured. Certain
of them said:

"We shall arrive too late. There will be no shining
and glorious feats of arms for us. They have already
entered into the city."

And they related to the King the noise and the
shouting which were heard, and how it seemed to
them that they had heard also the sounding of
trumpets.

"Verily," they said, "those who were there at the
moment of the attack had great good fortune; of all
the honour of this exploit they will always have the
better part."

At this moment the certain news was brought that
the gates of the city were passed, and that the Infantes
and the Count of Barcellos were there, fighting each
on his own.

I say nothing of the joy of the King Dom João;

albeit it was as great as you may conceive, he did
not at all betray it. For it was not in the character
of this king to betray his joy, even in the greatest
happiness, nor yet his sadness even in the greatest
misfortune. But he gazed at the lords who were there,
and he laughed when he knew how the Infante Dom
Duarte had gone secretly to join Dom Henrique, so
that he might be among the first in the assault upon
the city . . .

.   .   .

So soon as the signal to attack had been given to
this portion of the fleet all these men, who had waited
so long in impatience, rushed forward, full of an
extreme zeal, which was not by any means—and this
must be said—free from jealousy and envy; the nobles
would fain have been with those who were the first
to enter the city, for these would always have the
greatest glory and the greatest honour; and the
common people were stricken with grief to think that
their companions had already laid their hands on the
better part of the booty, and that for them would
remain only things without value.

Such was their haste that they very soon found
themselves within the city, and dividing themselves
into companies, Dom Pedro with his men, the
Constable with his, and so also the other lords, they
spread through the streets of Ceuta, fighting as best
they could, and they had much to do, for the city
was still filled with Moors who were defending it foot
by foot.

The King, well encompassed, sat himself down at
the gate of the city, remaining there for some while;
and this for two reasons: the first, because he was
wounded in one leg; and the second, because the city
was as good as taken, and it was not befitting his
condition to mingle in these combats until the time

for the attack upon the castle, which he wished to lead in person.   . . .

You may imagine the ardour of the combatants on either side. The din of battle was so great that there were many persons who said afterwards that it was heard at Gibraltar.

Some most noteworthy feats of arms were accomplished this day, very worthy of being recalled if they had come plainly to our knowledge; but you must think that there were there so many brave men, so numerous and so desirous of excelling, that nothing of all that passed was unworthy of being noted; all the more as the great slaughter which they worked among the Moors is testimony of this. But you must know the two reasons which prevented these exploits from being known as perfectly as they deserved: the first and the chiefest is in the fact that this battle was fought in the city itself, whose streets were so straight that those who were in the front rank could not be many, and those who followed them could not witness their exploits; the second reason was the time that has passed between these feats and the moment of writing them down; for, as I have said in the prologue to this history, the greater part of the nobles and persons of quality who were in this battle were already dead, and the others, those of the common sort, had no other care this day than theft, for they found on every hand the wherewithal to assuage their covetousness. And this was a thing very perilous, for that the houses had low and narrow doorways, according to the custom of the Moors. Those men who were led away by this heat of covetousness entered without

any prudence, which often caused their destruction,
for many of the Moors had taken refuge in their
houses and were defending them to the end, preferring
thus to lose their life rather than preserve it by taking
to flight . . . and seized by this grief (at losing their
homes and their city) they hid themselves behind the
doors in order to kill their enemies when these crossed
the threshold; but from this they had little advantage,
for behind the foremost were others, and they were
all armed . . . and the rage of the Moors was such
that at times, even without arms, they threw themselves upon the Christians; and their despair and their
fury were so great that they did not surrender themselves, even if they found themselves alone before a
multitude of enemies; and many of them, already
lying on the ground, and with their souls half severed
from their bodies, still made movements with their
arms as though they would deal mortal blows to
those who had vanquished them. Some of them took
their riches and threw them into the wells; others
buried them in the corners of their houses; for despite
the loss of their city they believed that they would
retake it afterwards, and would then be able to seek
their treasures there where they now hid them . . .

We have told how the Infante Dom Henrique
separated from his brother when the two assailed the
high places of the city. Dom Henrique, having lost
sight of his brother, made towards the street *Direita*
thinking to attempt the assault of the castle . . .

. . . The writer conceives that the Infante Dom
Henrique at this moment reasoned as follows:

"What matters it to me that I was the first captain
to whom the King, my lord, gave the order to leap

ashore and attack the city, since I have won the
victory with so little pains? And for what glory will
they be able to praise me on the day when I am
made knight, if my sword has not been dipped to
the hilt in the blood of the Infidels?"

Accompanied by this thought, he came to the street
Direita. He had been following it for some moments
when he saw a company of Christians who came
towards him, some five hundred, running and fleeing
before the Moors. The Infante lowered the vizor of
his casque and thrust his arm through the straps of
the buckler which he had not discarded. He let all
the Christians pass him; when the Moors came nigh
he flung himself upon them, and his blows were so
vigorous, and so swift and sure, that soon the Moors
recognized them among all the others which they
received; and in such wise that very soon they turned
on their heels and fled in their turn.

The Christians, having recognized the Infante, took
heart again, and turning upon the Moors pursued
them until they had come with them before the
houses where they unloaded the merchandise which
came from without, and which were called Dewan.
These houses had a gate which formed a barrier in
the direction of Almina. When the Moors had come
thither—perchance because they saw other Moors
who were coming to help them, or because it seemed
to them that the Portuguese were less furious in their
pursuit—they faced about and again attacked their
enemies, who retreated for the second time. The
Infante, who was then but twenty-one years of age,
and whose limbs were vigorous and his courage very
great, on seeing this was overcome with rage, and

running on the Moors assailed them so strongly that in the end he scattered them.

But the Christians were seized with such a fear that the greater number continued on their way and passed close to the Infante without seeing him. Those who remained fought bravely at the side of the Infante, and carried themselves so well that a goodly number of the Moors fell, and the others, unable to abide the combat, fled. The Infante, however, did not allow them to escape as before, but pursued them closely with his companions as far as the walls of the castle. And the course thus run was marked by the number of corpses that littered it . . .

. . . The Moors on reaching the walls of the castle found there some respite, for there are three walls in this place, the walls of the castle, and the other wall which divides the two sides of the city . . .

. . . Protected by these walls, which gave them shelter, and by the multitude of other Moors who were upon the walls and doing great injury to their enemies, they made ready to fight, all the more as they now perceived the small number of Christians who accompanied the Infante Dom Henrique, which gave them hope of an easy vengeance. For of those who had set out with the Infante after the Moors there were now no more than seventeen, since the others had little by little become scattered on the way; some drawn away by the lust to steal, others by thirst, for all their victuals were salt, and the great heat of the sun dried the moisture of their bodies and made them constantly seek the wells; others again were soft and frail by nature and could not very long support the fatigue of combats.

Thus, with the seventeen soldiers who were left him, the Infante had to support this desperate battle for two hours and a half. Under their blows many of the Moors were mortally wounded; and they in their turn wounded so sorely a squire of the Infante's, who was called Fernão Chamorro, that he fell to the ground without any semblance of life. The Moors strove to take him, but the Infante, and those who were with him, would by no means permit this. For a long while the struggle continued for the possession of this body upon the ground. And of a sudden the Infante attacked the Moors with such vigour and courage that they began to fall back; and the Christians always harassing them, they were forced to abandon this street and take refuge under the gate, the Infante still hard upon them and never ceasing to hew at them.

But of those seventeen who were with Dom Henrique in this adventure there were left no more than four . . .

. . . Who could have believed that the Infante, or a sole one of these four men, would escape such peril? Over this gate the wall was very thick and garnished with two rows of crenellations, in such sort that it was defended from above on either side. And there is also a tower with a vault which is pierced in divers places (for defence). In this tower is the second gate, which is round, and between this wall and the barrier is the passage leading to the third gate.

What would now befall? For the Moors whom they were driving before them were many, without counting the multitude who were upon the walls, and whose sole care was to prevent the entrance of the Christians. When these men saw that the Christians were entering as they fought, in a great mellay with their own people, they essayed to prevent them by casting stones upon them through the holes in the vault of the tower. But God willed that their desire should not be accomplished; and the Infante passed the gate, running before those Moors whom he had hitherto driven before him.

There are some who believe that the fact that they were so few in the accomplishment of this exploit was for the Christians one of the causes of their victory, for mingled as they were with this multitude of Moors, those on the walls feared by casting their weapons and projectiles to slay their own people. And so at length the Infante and his companions passed beyond the third gate . . .

. . .

This assault of the Infante's, and this hard and so unequal battle, which lasted for more than five hours without a moment's respite, determined the final victory of the Portuguese. When later, after many combats, the King commanded the assault upon the castle, those who entered it found it empty, for Salabensala had left the city.

How the great Mosque of Ceuta was dedicated to the worship of Our Lord, and how the Infantes were made knights and dukes by the King their father. How the Portuguese returned into their country leaving the City of Ceuta well guarded

O N the Wednesday following, the twenty-third day of the month, the King sent for the Master Fra João Xira and Affonso Eannes, his Grand Chaplain, and said to them:

"This next Sunday, if it please God, I wish to attend a solemn Mass with sermon in the great mosque of this city. Assemble, then, all my sons' chaplains and all the other priests who have come with the fleet, and make all the preparations needful for this end."

. . .

On the morrow the Grand Chaplain went to look at the mosque and busied himself in causing it to be cleaned, for the Moors, in order to prostrate themselves during their prayers, were wont to lay mats upon the pavement, which was very fine, and did not remove them, contenting themselves with laying new mats on those that were worn out; in such wise that a great depth of rubbish was thus formed, which had to be removed with the spade; and of this a great number of basketsful were taken out. After this the whole building was cleaned very thoroughly.

On the following day all the priests assembled in the mosque, wearing sumptuous priestly vestments, and in the presence of the King, the Infantes, and all the lords and nobles, who were clad with great magnificence, they proceeded to the exorcism over salt and water, with the ritual orisons of this act.

And when this ceremony was ended, they dedicated the temple to the service of Our Lord Jesus Christ and adorned it for the celebration of the Mass. When all was prepared the clergy sang in chorus *Te Deum Laudamus*, and the King gave the order to the trumpets to sound all together, and of them there were above two hundred . . .

. . . The Infante Dom Henrique called to mind that of old the Moors had carried away, from the city of Sines in Algarve, two church bells, and had search made for them. They found them, and were able to use them for the solemn Mass on Sunday.

On this occasion the Master Fra João Xira preached a very fine sermon.

Immediately after the Mass the Infantes withdrew to their apartments and donned their armour; and thus armed, they returned to the church.

. . .

. . . and this was a thing very fair to see, for they had all three tall bodies well built, and their armour was shining and richly ornamented, and their blessed swords hung from their belts . . . and before them marched the trumpets and the drums, in such sort that I do not believe there was a single man there who did not take great pleasure in beholding them, and, more than any other, he who was nearest to them, the King, their father.

And when they had come before him, first the Infante Dom Duarte fell to his knees, and, drawing his sword from the scabbard, gave it to him; and his father made him knight. And in the like fashion his two brothers were made knights after him. And when this was done all three kissed the King's hand, and went each his own way, and they in their turn made knights those of their train who had deserved it . . .

When all these ceremonies had been performed, the King assembled his Council, to decide the manner in which the city should be guarded after his departure. For it was to be foreseen that the Moors would ere long return and essay to recover their goodly lost city and the treasures that were in it. Day after day troops of Moors came before the city, and the Christians issued forth to fight with them and disperse them, and many men lost their lives there.

After many discussions, for opinions differed on certain points, the King resolved to confide the guard of the city of Ceuta to the Count Dom Pedro de Menezes. Many *fidalgos* asked leave of the King to remain in Ceuta with the Count; the King chose such as he wished to leave in this city, and, at their father's request, each of the Infantes chose among his servitors those who were to remain. And so, all counted, these gentlemen who remained under the orders of the Count Dom Pedro de Menezes were twenty to thirty; and reckoning the whole of the garrison that remained in Ceuta, the number of men was as many as two thousand seven hundred. And there was left also a sea captain with two galleys to guard the strait; and a great quantity of victuals, and armour, as well as swords, axes, lances, and arbalests, and other things needful for war; without counting the things that were found in the city and the dockyards; four galleys and a royal galley, and great plenty of darts, arrows, arbalests and bucklers; a bombard, much powder, tallow, wax, pitch, anchors, cordage, masts, tillers; and all this in very great abundance . . .

. . .

The second day of the month of September, a Monday, the whole fleet was ready to depart. All these *fidalgos* and squires came to the King to take leave of him. The King received them with much kindliness. He said to the Count Dom Pedro:

"Since God has inspired you with the desire to ask this of me [to remain in Ceuta as commander of the garrison] . . . I charge you always to have in your mind the responsibility which you have taken upon you, and in your heart the courage to guard, defend, and keep this city . . . and I recommend you also to protect and love these *fidalgos* whom I leave in your company to aid you . . . and I commend to you also all the other men who remain with you, and I require you to treat them with mildness and all the indulgence you may . . ."

And he told also the *fidalgos* that they must act always as if they were in his presence, and endeavour to increase their honour in all things, as befitted the lineage from which they were descended and the confidence which the King reposed in them. And they made answer to him that they would do always in such sort that the King would hear the news of their death before he would hear that they had failed in honour.

The ships that were to sail were ready; some had already hoisted their yards and were holding but by one anchor; others were sailing to and fro. So soon as the King entered into his galley he caused the signal to be given, and all the ships spread their sails and set out on their voyage to Algarve, sounding diversely the instruments of music which they had on board. For all the men were joyous. They rejoiced in the sweetness of victory, and the hope of presently seeing once more their country, their friends, and their kinsfolk.

But the others, who had remained in Ceuta, for the whole of that day did not leave the walls of the city, and had eyes only for the fleet that was departing. There were in this host of men those who wept as though they were sure that they would never again see their country and their friends. And in justice we shall say that it was not without reason that they had in their hearts such a longing for their home, for the place and the circumstances gave them true cause for melancholy . . .

. . . Certainly we ought not to blame them for thus betraying their sentiments, for this grief made them afterwards braver still and more furious against their enemies . . .

. . .

When the King had come to Tarifa, which is a city of Algarve, he sent for his sons, and he said to them:

"All good services deserve a reward. Not only because you are my sons, but because I have had from you very good service during the whole of this expedition, I desire that you should be rewarded. Firstly, I do not know what benefit I might grant my son the Infante Dom Duarte, it being the case that God has vouchsafed that he should be my eldest son and the heir of my kingdom and my territories; to him I will therefore say this: that even during my life he may take of these possessions what may please him. But you, my other two sons, I desire that you shall be dukes. You, Infante Dom Pedro, I make you Duke of Coimbra, and the Infante Dom Henrique shall be Duke of Vizeu; and him, for the greatness of his courage and the things that he has done, as well in the ordering of the fleet of Porto as during the assault of the city amidst so many fatigues and dangers, I make Senhor of Covilha."

The Infantes kissed his hand and gave him thanks. And he made them dukes with all the customary solemnities and ceremonies, for there were with them lords and nobles enough for the fitting celebration of such a festival . . .

The King largely rewarded all the lords who had accompanied him, and he also gave great largesse to those of the common people who had done well, each according to his trade. And all were content. From Algarve the King and the Infantes went first to Evora, where the Infanta Izabel received them, surrounded by noble ladies. And wherever they passed the people welcomed them with great joy.

And as for the manner in which they were received (throughout the country) and the joy of the people, I will not speak of them at greater length; for all those who shall read of the so virtuous deeds of this great prince (the King Dom João), and the pains he was at, and the exploits which he accomplished, for the safety and honour of his people, will well be able to conceive with what love he was welcomed wherever he passed, above all after winning so great a victory . . .

THE CHRONICLE OF THE DISCOVERY
OF GUINEA

EXTRACT FROM THE INTRODUCTION TO THE EDITION OF 1841

by THE VISCONDE DE SANTAREM

*T*HE *Chronicle of the Discovery of Guinea* was written by a contemporary. It is one of the most valuable monuments of the history of the Portuguese discoveries and conquests, and it is also the first book written by a European concerning the regions situated on the western coast of Africa, beyond Cape Bojador. It was believed, until well on in the nineteenth century, that the oldest chronicler to write of the Infante Dom Henrique, and of his labours and discoveries, was a foreigner, the celebrated Italian traveller Cadomosto, who came to Portugal and entered the service of the Infante about the year 1455. *The Chronicle of the Discovery of Guinea*, however, was completed in 1448. It seems that the Portuguese King Dom Affonso V (nephew of the Infante Dom Henrique) presented it to his uncle the King of Naples, Alfonso the Magnanimous, about 1453–7. At the beginning of the eighteenth century this chronicle of Azurara's was in Spanish hands. Ferdinand Denis found it in 1837 in Paris, in the Bibliothèque Nationale, where it still remains.[1] This original text is a small folio written on parchment, and sumptuously executed. It contains 319 pages and 622 columns, and a miniature of the Infante Dom Henrique, painted during his lifetime: the only authentic portrait of this prince. His head is

---

[1] F. Denis made it known to the public in his book: *Chroniques Chevaleresques de l'Espagne et du Portugal*, Paris, 1839, vol. ii, pp. 43–53.

covered with a great black hat; he wears no insignia; and his hair is cut short in token of mourning, as was the custom of the period. His brother, the Infante Dom Pedro, Duke of Coimbra, had not long been dead.

The Visconde de Carreira, Minister Plenipotentiary of Portugal in France, immediately obtained from the French Government its authorization to publish this chronicle. He copied it with his own hand,[1] and the proofs were corrected by a Portuguese philologist. It was published in 1841 (J. P. Ailland, Paris) in an *édition de luxe*, having as its frontispiece a facsimile of the miniature of the Infante.

Azurara's fidelity as historian is incontestable. His scruples as chronicler, and his love of truth, were such that being sometimes unable to obtain absolutely exact data concerning the termination of certain events which he was engaged in recounting, he preferred to leave his narrative uncompleted. His authority as a contemporary writer is very great, for he lived in intimate relations with the Infante Dom Henrique, and he knew personally the leading captains to whom the world owed the discoveries of this period, and of whom almost all were the servitors of the Infante, instructed in the sciences under this prince's direction.

[1] The notes to this chronicle are also from the pen of the Visconde de Santarem, being reprinted from the edition of 1841.

THE WEST COAST OF AFRICA

Portuguese Chart of the Sixteenth Century.—*From the Atlas known as the
Duchesse de Berry's Atlas. B.N. Res. Ge FF* 14409

CHAPTER I

*How Azurara speaks of the Infante Dom Henrique
before beginning his tale of the discovery of Guinea*

IT seems to me that I should write overmuch if I
had to recount in full all the particularities which
some historians are wont to write down concerning
the princes of whom they are speaking. Thus, in
relating what these princes have done, seized by the
desire to exalt their virtues, they begin the history of
their lives at the time of their earliest infancy. And
although one may think that writers so capable must
have good reasons for so doing, as for me I shall
depart from this procedure, recognizing that in
respect of my present subject it would be a labour
hardly necessary. I do not propose to discourse at
great length even concerning his bodily aspect, for
there have been many persons in this world with
features in good proportion, yet their offences against
honesty did violence to their renown; and for the
rest, what the philosopher has said on this subject will
suffice us—that corporeal beauty is not a perfect good.
And thus, returning to my subject, I say that this
noble prince was of middle stature, a man thickset,
with limbs large and powerful, and bushy hair; the
skin was white, but the travail and the battles of life
altered its hue as time went on. His aspect, to those
who beheld him for the first time, was severe; when
anger carried him away—rarely—his countenance
became terrifying. He had force of mind and acute
intelligence in a high degree. His desire to accomplish

great deeds was beyond all comparison. Lust and avarice had never obtained a hold upon his heart, for as to the first of these vices, he was so moderate that all his life he preserved the most perfect chastity, and his body was virgin when it was laid in the earth. What shall I say of his magnificence, which was extreme among all the princes of the world! To my thinking, he was the uncrowned prince who had in his household the greatest number of servants, and of the finest quality. His house gave welcome to all men of the realm who possessed merit, and even more to foreigners whose renown justified the expense he was at to have them there; for as an ordinary thing he had about him men of different countries; men of very distant countries, and all held him for a great marvel; and never departed without receiving great benefits from him. All his days were filled with assiduous labour; for surely among all the nations of mankind one could not find any more able than he to subdue himself. It would be hard indeed to count the nights during which his eyes knew no sleep, and his body so mortified itself that it seemed to make a new nature for itself. The continuance of his labour was such that, even as the poets figured Atlas, the giant sustaining the heavens on his shoulders, because of his great knowledge of the celestial bodies, so the people of our realm held it for a maxim that the great labours of this prince surpassed the summits of the loftiest mountains. I shall say that things which seemed impossible to men were rendered easy by the persistence of his effort. He was a man of excellent counsel, and of great authority, wise and possessed of a faithful memory, but slow in certain things, perchance because his character was something phlegmatic, or because such was his will in a certain purpose of which those about him were ignorant. He was quiet in manner, and his words were calm; in adversity he was constant, and humble in prosperity. It is very sure that no other prince has ever had vassal like unto him, or who could even be compared with him, in obedience and veneration, such as he showed to the kings who in his time reigned over Portugal; above all to King Dom Affonso, his nephew, during the early part of his reign, as you may see more clearly by this chronicle. Never was known in him hatred or ill-will toward any, even though heavy faults were committed against him, and in this point his bounty was such that competent men reproached him with weakness in the dispensing of justice, for he judged all alike. And they thought so because on certain of his servants, who abandoned him during the siege of Tangier, which was the most perilous adventure that ever he was engaged in, he inflicted no punishment; not only did he receive them back again, but he gave them great privileges, more than to others who had served him well, while according to the judgment of men the first were far from deserving what they had received. This is the only weakness which I have found it possible to relate of him . . .

. . . He drank wine only during a very short period of his life, and this was in his early youth; but afterwards, all his life long, he drank none. He had always a great love for the commonwealth of this kingdom, dedicating thereto a large part of his labours, and it pleased him to make trial of novelties for the

general good, even devoting great expenditure to
them; he gave himself with much delight to the
exercise of arms, especially against the enemies of the
holy faith; and he desired peace with all Christians.
He was generally loved by all, for he did good to all
and harm to none. His replies were always courteous,
which honoured the condition of the persons who
spoke to him without abating his own. Never did
lewd or unhandsome word issue from his mouth. He
was obedient to all the commands of Holy Church,
and attended her offices with great devotion; in his
chapel these offices were performed with as much
solemnity and ceremony as in the chancel of no
matter what cathedral. And also he cherished a great
veneration for all sacred things, and honoured their
ministers and loaded them with benefits. He fasted
almost half the year, and the poor never left his
presence with empty hands. Assuredly I could not
find another Catholic or religious man, whether prince
or no, who could compare with him. His heart never
knew fear other than the fear of sin, and because
high exploits are born of virtuous works and righteous
customs, I shall assemble in the following chapter all
the noteworthy things which he accomplished in the
service of God and for the honour of the realm.

. . .

I shall not find a better opening for this chapter
than the recital of the remarkable conquest of the
great city of Ceuta, a celebrated victory which
glorified the heavens and favoured the earth. For it
seems to me that there was enough glory for the
college of celestial virtues in all the divine sacrifices
and sacred ceremonies which until this day have been

performed in this city in honour of Jesus Christ our Lord, and which, by His divine grace, will continue to be performed. As for the profit which the earth has received thereby, the Levant and the Ponent[1] are sure witnesses, for their inhabitants can now exchange their merchandise without great danger to their goods; and it cannot be denied that the city of Ceuta is the key of the whole Mediterranean Sea.

In this conquest the Infante Dom Henrique was the captain of a very great and very powerful fleet, and, as a valiant knight, he fought all that day on which the city was taken from the Moors. Under his command were the Count of Barcellos, bastard of the King, and Dom Fernando, lord of Bragança, his nephew, and Gonçalo Vasques Coutinho, who was a very puissant seigneur, and also many other *fidalgos*, with all their men, and yet others who joined them, from these provinces, which is to say from Beira, Traz os Montes, and betwixt Douro and Minho.

The first royal captain who touched land near the walls of Ceuta was he of whom I write, and his square banner was the first to pass the gates of the city, the Infante himself being not far from its shadow. And the blows he dealt the enemy that day were noteworthy among all others, since for five hours he fought without respite, and neither the heat, which was great, nor the fatigue of such an effort could persuade him to depart and take some rest . . .

And in this city the Infante was knighted, with much honour, by the hands of his father on the

[1] Levant, Ponent: the quarters in which the sun rises and sets respectively, i.e. East, West. (B. M.)

day the cathedral was consecrated, as well as his brothers.

The capture of this city took place on a Thursday, August 31, 1415. And on returning into his kingdom the King Dom João, in a certain place in Algarve, confirmed the prince in the dignity of duke, with the seigneurie (of this domain).

At the end of three years a great multitude of Moors came down upon the city of Ceuta; the *alfaqueques*[1] afterwards found that there were a hundred thousand of them; for there were the people of the King of Fez, the King of Granada, the King of Tunis, the King of Morocco, and the King of Bugia, with great quantities of engines and artillery, in the intent to recapture this city by besieging it on land and sea.

The Infante Dom Henrique, with his two brothers, Dom João and the Count of Barcellos, who afterwards became the Duke of Bragança, came to the succour of the city, with many other lords and *fidalgos*, and a great fleet. And having accomplished a great carnage among the Moors, he quickly freed the city, repaired it, and returned victoriously into Portugal; not well content, however, for the circumstances did not allow him to take the city of Gibraltar as he had thought to do, and the chief cause of this was the severity of the winter which was beginning; for the sea was perilous everywhere at this time of the year, and more so than ever in this place, by reason of the strong tides which are there.

The Infante went also with a great fleet to the

---

[1] An Arabic word signifying he who redeems captives, who liberates slaves and prisoners of war; and also courier, and perhaps spy.

Canary Isles, in order to lead their inhabitants into the path of the holy faith.

And afterwards, during the reign of the King Dom Duarte, and by his order, the Infante went the third time into Africa, where he laid siege to the city of Tangier, and installed himself in the territories of his enemies in nineteen places, with his banners unfurled. The siege lasted twenty-two days, and great exploits were accomplished there, worthy of being recalled, and with great loss to his enemies, as you will see in the Chronicle of the realm.

The Infante Dom Henrique governed Ceuta for thirty-five years[1] by order of the king, his father, his brother, and his nephew, with so much wisdom and skill that the crown of the realm always derived honour therefrom, and at length, by reason of his great labours, he left the government of Ceuta to his nephew the King Dom Affonso at the beginning of his reign.

After the taking of Ceuta the Infante had ships at sea armed against the Infidels, whom he fought, and upon whom he did much ravage, and this on the two coasts, in such sort that the terror of his enemies gave security to the countries neighbouring on our Spain, and still more to the merchants who traded from the Levant to the Ponent.

He caused to be peopled five islands in the great ocean, which islands, at the time this book was composed, were already sufficiently populated; above all the island of Madeira; and from this, as also from the others, the realm had great profit in bread [wheat],

[1] "He governed" means that the Infante had supreme control of the affairs of Ceuta, but not that he lived there.

sugar, honey, wax and wood, and many other things, from which not only our realm, but also foreigners, derived great profit.

.   .   .

And since I have begun this chapter with the taking of a city, I will complete it by speaking of the town which this prince caused to be built upon Cape San Vincente, where the two seas meet in conflict: which is to say, the great Ocean and the Mediterranean Sea. Of the perfections of this town I cannot speak at length, for at the time when this book was written it had as yet only its walls, which were those of a strong fortress, with a few houses, but they were toiling at it without respite, and according to the current opinion, the Infante wished to build there a special town for the traffic of the merchants, and so that all ships passing from the Levant to the Ponent might anchor there, and find victuals and pilots, as they do at Cadiz, whose harbour is greatly inferior to this . . .

And I have heard it said that so soon as the building of this town was begun the Genoese made offer to acquire it for a great price. And the Genoese, as you know, are people who do not make employ of their money without great hope of gain.

Although other names have been given to this town, I believe that its true name, according to the intention of him who caused it to be built, is *City of the Infante*, for he himself named it thus, as well in speaking as in writing.[1]

.   .   .

[1] It was called first *Tercena Naval*, from the Venetian word *Darcena*, arsenal (of galleys). Then *Villa do Infante*, and subsequently *Sagres*.

. . . How many times did the rising sun find him seated where it had left him the day before, waking all the hours of the night, without a moment of repose, surrounded by people of divers nationalities, not without profit to each of them, since for him there was no greater pleasure than to find the way to give this profit to all! Where will you find another human body capable of supporting, as his in battle, the fatigues from which he had so little repose in time of peace! Certainly I believe that if strength could be represented, its veritable form would be found in the countenance and limbs of this prince, for it was not only in certain things that he showed himself to be strong, but in all. And what strength is there greater than that of the man who is conqueror of himself? He supported hunger and thirst in a manner hardly credible . . .

. . . Fortunate prince, the honour of our realm, what matter was there in your life which those who write your praises could pass over in silence; what point, what moment of your time was poor in benefits or empty of merit? I think of the manner in which you welcomed all, how you gave ear to all, how you passed the greater part of your days and nights, employed in so many labours and cares, in order that many people might profit thereby; and I see how the land and the seas are full of your name; for by continual efforts you have united the Levant with the Ponent, so that men may learn to exchange their wealth. In truth, I have already spoken many things of you, but very many more remain to be said . . .

I

CHAPTER II

The reasons which led the Infante to seek the lands of Guinea; how this enterprise was begun, and how Gil Eannes was the first to round Cape Bojador

WE consider that we know things when we know him who has accomplished them and the object for which they were accomplished. In the foregoing chapters we have shown you the Infante Dom Henrique as chief artisan of these things in making him known to you as well as was in our power; and in this chapter it is proper that you should know why he accomplished these things.

You must take good note that the magnanimity of this prince constrained him always to begin, and lead to a good conclusion, high exploits; and for this reason, after the taking of Ceuta, he had always at sea ships armed against the Infidels. And because he desired to know what lands there were beyond the Canary Isles and a cape which was called Bojador, for up to that time no one knew, whether by writing or the memory of any man, what there might be beyond this cape.

Some believed that St. Brandan[1] had passed it; others said that two galleys had gone thither and had never returned. But it seems to us that this cannot be in any way true, for it is not credible that if the said galleys had gone thither, other ships would not

[1] The Voyage of St. Brandan, of which the author is speaking here, is considered to be as fabulous as the island of that name. According to this tradition St. Brandan landed on the island, lying on the Equator, in A.D. 565.

have undertaken to discover what had become of them. And the Infante Dom Henrique desired to know the truth of this; for it seemed to him that if he or some other lord did not essay to discover this, no sailor or merchant would undertake this effort, for it is very sure that these do not think to navigate otherwhere than to places where they already know that they will find their profit. And seeing that no other prince was concerning himself with the matter, he sent his own ships to these countries in order to acquire certitude, and this for the service of God and of the King Dom Duarte, his brother and seigneur, who was reigning at this time. And this was the first reason of his enterprise.

And the second was the thought that if in these territories there should be any population of Christians, or any harbours where men could enter without peril, they could bring back to the realm many merchandises at little cost, by reason that there would be no other persons on these coasts who would negotiate with them; and that in like manner one could carry to these regions merchandise of the realm, of which the traffic would be of great profit to the natives.

The third reason was founded on this: that it was said that the power of the Moors of this land of Africa was very much greater than was generally thought, and that there were among them neither Christians nor other races. And because every wise man is moved by desire to know the strength of his enemy, the Infante devised means to send his people in quest of information, in order to know the full extent of the Infidels' power.

The fourth reason was this: during one and thirty years of battles with the Moors the Infante had never found Christian king or seigneur, outside this kingdom, who, for the love of Our Lord Jesus Christ, was willing to aid him in this war. He desired to know whether in those regions there might be any Christian princes in whom the charity and love of Christ were strong enough to cause them to aid him against these enemies of the faith.

The fifth reason was his great desire to increase the holy faith in Our Lord Jesus Christ, and to lead to this faith all souls desirous of being saved, recognizing that the whole mystery of the Incarnation, the death, and the passion of Our Lord Jesus Christ took place to this end: namely, that lost souls should be saved; and the Infante was fain, by his efforts and his expenditure, to lead these souls into the true path, understanding that man could render the Lord no greater service. For if God has promised a hundred treasures in return for one, it is just that we should believe that for so many treasures—which is to say, for so many souls which were saved by the agency of this prince—there would be in the Kingdom of God as many hundreds of rewards, which would permit his soul, after this life, to be glorified in the celestial kingdom. For myself, who am writing this history, I have seen so many men and women of these regions converted to the holy faith that, even if this prince were pagan, the prayers of these men and women would be enough to save him. And I have seen not only these people, but also their children and their grandchildren; and they had all become true Christians, as though the Divine grace were awaiting in them the moment when they were given clear knowledge of themselves.

The writer concludes this chapter with a sixth reason, from which, it seems to him, all the others proceed : the astrological reason, on which he enlarges, giving copious explanations, finally arriving at the conclusion that, according to the disposition of the planets :

. . . this prince was bound to engage in great and noble conquests, and above all was he bound to attempt the discovery of things which were hidden from other men, and secret . . . and all his exploits and conquests would be loyally accomplished, giving full satisfaction to his King and seigneur.

The Infante Dom Henrique, having completed his preparations in his town of Sagres, began to send his caravels and his men along the western coast of Africa, with the mission of rounding Cape Bojador, and bringing back word to him as to what they found beyond this limit, which no man until then had passed.   . . .

. . . However, although many set out—and they were men who had won fair renown by their exploits in the trade of arms—none dared go beyond this cape . . .

And this, to tell truth, was not by reason of any lack of courage or goodwill, but because they had to do with a thing entirely novel, which was yet mingled with ancient legends which had existed for generations among the mariners of the Spains. And although these legends were deceitful, the idea of discovering if they were true seemed full of menace; and it was doubtful who would be the first to be willing to risk his life in such an adventure.

"How shall we pass beyond the limits established by our elders?" they said. "What profit can the Infante win from the loss of our souls and our bodies? for plainly we should be as men taking their own lives. Have there not been in the Spains other princes or lords as desirous as the Infante of knowing these things? It is very sure that among so many such noble princes and lords, who have accomplished such high exploits, by which their memories are honoured, some one of them all must have had the thought of such an enterprise. But assuredly perceiving the peril, and no hope of honour or profit, he ceased to think of it. This is clear, said the mariners; beyond this cape there is no one, there is no population; the land is no less sandy than the deserts of Libya, where is no water at all, neither trees nor green herbs; and the sea is so shallow that at a league from the shore its depth is hardly a fathom. The tides are so strong that the ships which pass the cape will never be able to return[1] . . ."

. . . This dread was great in these mariners, threatened not alone by fear but by the shadow of fear. And this was the cause of great expense, since

[1] These notions were gathered from the works of the ancient geographers and the accounts of those Moors who crossed the great desert in caravans. This chapter shows us also how strong was the influence, at this period, of the traditions of the Arab geographers relating to the *Mare Tenebrosum*, which, according to them, lay beyond the isles of Kalidad (Canaries) which were situated at the extremity of the Mogreb. See Edrisi, Backoui, and Ebn-al-Ourdi.

Concerning the dread felt by the mediaeval navigators, see the *Itinera Mundi* of Abraham PERITSOL, translated from the Hebrew into Latin by HYDE.

for twelve years the Infante continued his effort, sending his ships to these regions each year, with great expense to his revenue; and none of these ships dared to go beyond the cape, although they returned with honour, since to make up for the fact that they had not accomplished the mission with which their lord had charged them, some of them descended upon the coast of Granada, and others sailed upon the sea of the Levant until they made great capture of Infidels, with which they returned honourably to the kingdom.   . . .

. . . The Infante always welcomed with great patience the captains of the ships which he had sent to seek out these countries, never showing them any resentment, listening graciously to the tale of their adventures, and rewarding them as those who were serving him well. And immediately he sent them back again to make the same voyage, them or others of his household, upon his armed ships, insisting more and more strongly upon the mission to be accomplished, and promising each time greater rewards to those who should bring him the intelligence he desired.

And at last, after twelve years of effort, the Infante had a barque fitted out, appointing the captain his squire Gil Eannes, whom he afterwards knighted and rewarded largely. This captain made the same voyage that the others had made, and overcome by the same dread did not pass beyond the Canary Isles, where he took captives, and returned to the kingdom. And this took place in the year 1433 of Jesus Christ. But the following year the Infante again had the same barque fitted out, and sending for Gil Eannes, and speaking with him alone, he recommended him strongly to do all that was possible to go beyond the cape; and that even if he did no more on this voyage, that would seem to him sufficient.

"You cannot meet there a peril so great," said the Infante, "that the hope of reward shall not be even greater. In truth, I marvel at these imaginings which have possessed you all, and of matters so uncertain. If these things possessed any authority, even though that authority were small, I might still find excuse for you; but I am astonished to think that you have them from the opinion of some few mariners who know only the navigation of Flanders and other ports to which they are accustomed to resort, and do not know how to handle a compass or make use of a chart of the seas. Have, therefore, no fear of their opinion in undertaking your voyage, because, with the grace of God, you shall derive therefrom only honour and profit."

The Infante was possessed of great authority; his remonstrances, even the lightest, were for wise men of great weight. And this was proved on this occasion, for having heard these words Gill Eannes promised himself resolutely that he would never again appear before his lord without having accomplished the mission with which he had been charged. And it was even so, for on this voyage, disdaining all peril, he passed beyond the cape, where he found matters very different from what he and others had imagined . . .

· · ·

And on his return he related to the Infante how the voyage had passed; having lowered a small boat into the sea, he had approached the shore and had landed without finding any person or sign of population. "And because it seemed to me," said Gil Eannes, "that I ought to bring back some token of this country, since I was there, I gathered these plants, which in our kingdom we call roses of St. Mary."

He having thus related to the Infante the account of his voyage, the Infante straightway had a *barinal*[1] fitted out, in which he sent Affonso Gonçalves Baldaya, his cup-bearer, and also Gil Eannes, in his caravel, commanding them to return thither, as indeed they did; and they found lands without habitations, but with imprints of the feet of men and camels.[2] And because such were the orders they had received, or of necessity, they returned with this news, without having done any other thing worthy of being recounted.

[1] A sort of galley.

[2] The Portuguese sailors gave this bay the name of *Bahia dos Ruivos*, because of the great quantity of these fish which they found there. This bay, so named, is marked on the map of Africa in the Portuguese atlas of the sixteenth century which may be seen in the Bibliothèque Nationale of Paris (*R.B.* No. 764).

How the Portuguese discovered the African coast as far as Cape Blanco and the bay and islands of Arguin; and the first captives whom they brought back from those parts

"SINCE matters are thus," said the Infante to Affonso Gomes Baldaya, "since you have found imprints of the feet of men and camels, it seems to me that there must be some population not far remote; or perchance there are people who go with their merchandise to some seaport where ships can anchor and receive merchandise; for since there are men, even if they are very wild, they must engage in seafaring matters, or at least in fisheries. Thus my intent is to send you anew on this same *barinal*; and as much to render me service as for your own honour, I charge you to go as far as is possible, and to do your best to contrive to speak with these people, or to take some of them, for it would be a great thing, and according to my desire, to have some person of these countries who could give me intelligence."

The boat was quickly armed, and Affonso Gonçalves set forth, very desirous of contenting the Infante. And pursuing their voyage, they ran seventy leagues beyond the place to which they had come the last time, which is to say, one hundred and twenty leagues beyond the cape; where they found a bay that seemed the mouth of a great river, in which there were very good anchorages, and whose entrance indented the

PROBABLE APPEARANCE OF A CARAVEL IN THE DAYS OF THE
INFANTE DOM HENRIQUE

Painting by Gregorio Lopes, early sixteenth century, from the retable of
St. Aute in the Convent of Madre de Deus.—*Lisbon, Museum of Ancient Art*

coast to a depth of eight leagues. And there they cast their anchors.[1]

Affonso Gonçalves had on board two horses which the Infante had given him. He had them immediately disembarked, and commanded two young men to mount them and ride into the interior of the country as far as they might; looking well on every hand, and essaying to discover some inhabitants or people who might be following some path. And in order that they should be the less fatigued, and also the horses, he recommended them to carry no defensive armour, but only their swords and lances, in order to attack if need were, for if they should meet with people who should wish to take them, their best remedy would be the legs of the horses, unless they found some person alone, from whom without peril they could derive some profit.

And these two young men showed, in the accomplishment of their mission, what men they would become later; for they were very far from their native country and all alone, without knowing what folk nor in what numbers they were going to encounter; without fear of wild beasts, the sole thought of which might have disquieted them like a terrifying shadow, for they were both young, neither being over twenty-six years of age.

Howbeit, despite all these considerations, they set forth with great courage, covering seven leagues of the bank of this river, until they beheld nineteen men gathered together, without other weapons of attack

[1] The Portuguese gave this bay the name of *Angra dos Cavollos* (Bay of the Horses). This bay, so named, is marked on almost all the maps of Africa dating from the sixteenth and seventeenth centuries.

or defence than javelins. And immediately the two young men saw them they rushed upon them. But in spite of their numbers these men dared by no means give them battle in the open field, and ran toward the cover of some rocks, where they fought for some considerable time with the Portuguese. And during this fight one of them was wounded in one foot; but although slight, his wound did not remain unavenged, for he wounded also one of the enemy. This fight continued until the sun announced the approach of night; and for this reason the Portuguese then returned to the ship . . .

. . .

Afterwards I made the acquaintance of one of these youths; he was *fidalgo*, very valiant in the trade of arms, and was called Heitor Homem: in the chronicle of the kingdom you will find him, giving his measure in goodly exploits. The other was called Diogo Lopes d'Almeida, *fidalgo*, and a man of great valour according to the thinking of people who knew him and spoke of him to me.

They then returned to the ship, as I have said, reaching it towards the dawn, and resting awhile. And at break of day Affonso Gonçalves fitted out his ship's boat, in which he embarked with a few men, ascending the river and despatching the two young men on horseback along the bank to the place where they had left the Moors the night before; and it was the intention of Affonso Gonçalves to fight them and take some of them prisoner. But his effort was fruitless, for the Moors had taken fright and had fled, leaving their poor possessions, with which Affonso Gonçalves charged his boat; not because of their value, but in testimony of this fact. And seeing that he would gain nothing by going further, he returned to the ship.

At the mouth of the river he saw upon a sandbank a great multitude of sea-wolves;[1] according to the reckoning of some, they were as many as five thousand. Of these he had slaughtered as many as might be, and loaded his boat with their pelts . . .

. . . But Affonso Gonçalves was not content, for he had not been able to take any of the Moors; and he sailed fifty leagues farther (along the coast) in the hope of laying hands on a man, or even a woman or child, to satisfy his master's desire. And thus he arrived at a point of land where there was a rock, which from afar was like a galley, and for this reason the name of *Porto da Galé* was given to this harbour.[2] There they disembarked and found nets, which they took. And here must be noted a new thing for us who live in the Spains; it is the thread of which these nets are made, for it is furnished by the bark of a tree so fitted for this end that without other preparation or admixture of flax it can be spun, and nets and all sorts of cordage can be made of it.

After this Affonso Gonçalves returned to Portugal, without learning whether these men were Moors or Gentiles, or what was their manner of living. And this took place in the year of Jesus Christ 1436.

During the following years the voyages along the western coast of Africa were to some extent relinquished. The Infante took part in the siege of Tangier,

[1] *Phoca vitulina*, Linn.
[2] Marked in the Portuguese atlas of the sixteenth century now in the Bibliothèque Nationale, and in the Venetian charts of Gastaldi (1564).

and in the year 1438 the King Dom Duarte died, leaving the heir to the throne at a tender age. Disorders followed, two parties being formed; one for the Queen and the other for the Infante Dom Pedro. And Dom Henrique, whose prudence and authority were recognized, had much ado to restore peace and prevent a civil war. At length Dom Pedro was made regent of the realm during the minority of his nephew the Prince Dom Affonso, and the Infante Dom Henrique was able once more to engage in his maritime enterprises.

None the less, in the meantime ships had sailed almost every year for the western coast of Africa. But some of them had to suffer contrary winds, and others went only to the Rio do Ouro in quest of the pelts and oil of seals.

. . .

. . . And thus in this year of 1441, the affairs of the kingdom being already more settled, although this tranquillity was not as yet very great, the Infante Dom Henrique fitted out a small vessel, appointing as its captain a certain Antão Gonçalves, his officer of the wardrobe, a man somewhat young in years; and the aim of this voyage was not other, according to the orders of the shipmaster, than to seek the pelts and oil of those sea-wolves of which we spoke in another chapter. There is no doubt, however, that the Infante had given him the same recommendations as to the other captains, but by reason of his age and his scant authority the recommendation was assuredly less forcible, and so the hope of success very much slighter.

When the chief mission of this voyage was accomplished Antão Gonçalves called upon Affonso Gonçalves, another young servitor of the Infante's household who was with him, and also the other men of the ship, who were in all twenty-one, and spoke to them thus: "Brothers and friends, we have already our whole cargo, as you may see, and thus our chief mission is accomplished, and we can return to our own country, if we have no longing to do more than that which was given us as our chief task. But I would know first of all if it seems good to you that we essay to achieve somewhat that will prove our goodwill to him who sent us; for it seems to me that it would be a shameful thing to return into his presence having done so little to serve him . . .

". . . I am going to tell you what I have devised in my mind, in order that you may tell me your opinion of it. This night, with nine of you, those who are the most disposed to undertake this advantage, I wish to go ashore and march along the bank of this river, so that we may endeavour to find some people; for it seems to me that we shall find them, since there are those who travel with camels and other animals which carry their goods. And their trafficking must be mainly in the direction of the sea. And since they do not yet know of our presence, they should not be united in such great numbers that we could not essay their strength. And the least victory which we could achieve will be to capture one of them, which will give great joy to the Infante our lord, for from his person he will be able to obtain knowledge regarding the other inhabitants of these countries . . ."

. . . And the others resolved to do according to his desire, and to follow him as far as their strength would permit. When it was night Antão Gonçalves chose the nine who seemed to him the most able, and with them he undertook the journey upon which he had resolved.

At a league from the sea they came upon a path, and to this they kept, thinking that some man or woman would pass along it whom they could capture. But it did not so fall out, and for this reason Antão Gonçalves said to the others that they would have to go still farther in pursuit of their end; and since they were so disposed, it would not be good to return to the ship with empty hands. The others agreeing, they set off toward the interior of the country, and they marched three leagues and found the imprints of the feet of men and children, whose number seemed to them to be forty or fifty, and they were following the path in the contrary direction to that which they were following themselves. It was very hot, and by reason of this heat, and their waking all night and travelling so long afoot, and having no water to drink, Antão Gonçalves understood that their fatigue was already too great, which he could judge by the degree of his own.

"Friends," he said, "there is nothing to be done here; our fatigue is great, and I do not see the profit of pursuing this path; for these men have gone towards the place from which we come, and the best thing we can do is to return upon our steps. It may be that in this manner we shall encounter them as they return, perchance in separate companies, or at some moment when they are resting. We shall attack them shrewdly; it may be that they will flee, but there will be at least some less nimble runners among them, whom we shall be able to capture, or perchance we shall have better fortune, and fall upon some fourteen or fifteen of them, of whom we shall make a more advantageous capture."

This counsel could not be debated, since it expressed the desire of all. They accordingly turned back toward the sea, and they had not been marching long before they saw a man, all naked, who was leading a camel, holding two javelins in his hand. The Portuguese set off in his pursuit, and at this moment none of them felt fatigue. Although he was alone and perceived that the others were many, he wished to show that he honoured his weapons, and began to defend himself as best he might. Affonso Goterres wounded him with a thrust of his lance; the Moor was dismayed by this wound, and threw his weapon to the ground like a man vanquished. They straightway made him their prisoner, and joyfully continued on their way. They then perceived upon a hill the people whose footprints they were following, of whose number was the man whom they had taken. They were very desirous of attacking them, but the sun was sinking, and their fatigue was extreme; they thought that this enterprise might bring them more scathe than profit, and resolved to return to their ship. And as they were moving off they saw coming a black woman who was a servant to those who were on the hill. The counsel of some was to leave her in peace, for her capture in the face of those to whom she belonged, and whose number was at least twice as great as their own, might lead to some skirmish, for these people would surely not suffer to see enemies take that which belonged to them. But Antão Gonçalves said that they ought to take her, for the very reason that this offence would perchance

K

induce those who were on the hill to come and encounter them. And as the orders of a captain, for those who are accustomed to obey, have great authority, the Morisco woman was taken.

Upon this, those who were on the hill[1] essayed to come to her aid, but seeing that our men were ready to receive them, not only did they withdraw as far as the hill, but they turned their backs and fled.

. . .

We are to learn now that Nuno Tristão, a young knight who had been reared from childhood in the household of the Infante, came to this place where Antão Gonçalves was. He came in an armed caravel, and he had orders from his lord to go beyond Porto da Galé, as far as ever he could, and to do his utmost to take captives in whatever manner he found possible.

. . .

When Tristão heard the adventure of Antão Gonçalves and his companions he resolved that he would go no farther before he had essayed, in this same place, where they now knew that there were inhabitants, to secure a larger haul of captives; for he well knew the Infante's desire to see and question the natives of these countries, in order to obtain from them the information which he had been seeking in vain for fifteen years, at the cost of such travail and expense. The two young captains, Nuno Tristão and Antão Gonçalves, resolved accordingly to set forth that very night toward the interior, taking each ten men, chosen from among their companions, in order to discover and pursue those people whom Antão Gonçalves had seen on the hill.

---

[1] This hill is marked on the unpublished maps in the Bibliothèque Nationale of Paris; it is situated to the south of the Rio do Ouro.

. . . And they were so favoured by chance that in the dark of the night they came to a place where lay some natives, who were divided into two camps; the distance between these camps was not great, so that our men divided themselves into three groups, the better to encircle them, for they were not very sure of the position of the camps; they felt it rather; for you know very well that these things are felt more clearly in the night than by day. And so soon as they were near enough they cast themselves upon them, shouting "Portugal and Santiago!" by which the natives were so surprised that they dispersed dismayed, and fled in disorder.

Nevertheless, the men defended themselves with their javelins, for they knew nothing of the use of other weapons; one of them who fought with Nuno Tristão defended himself until the captain killed him; and three others were killed besides; and ten taken—men, women, and children. Among the prisoners was a tall man who was called Adahu, whom they said was a knight, and whose aspect plainly showed the nobility which made him superior to the rest . . .

. . .

. . . This feat being accomplished, the Portuguese who had taken part in the fighting assembled together and manifested their desire to see Antão Gonçalves knighted, as to which he was by no means willing, saying that he ought not to receive so great an honour for so small an exploit; all the more as he was too young, and did not wish to become knight before he had furnished other proofs of his merit. At length, because the others persisted in their request, and because Nuno Tristão held that they were in the right, this captain knighted Antão Gonçalves, albeit against his will. For which reason this place was called *Porto do Cavalleiro*;[1] and he was the first to be made knight in this region.

When these captains had returned to their ships they commanded a Bedouin Arab[2] whom Nuno Tristão had brought with him to endeavour to converse with the captives; but the latter did not understand him, for their language is not Moorish, but the *azenague*[3] of *Zaara*,[4] which is the name by which this country is known.

However, the knight who was among the captives, because he was a nobleman among his own people, had more knowledge of affairs than the others, and had travelled in other countries, where he had learned the Moorish language; and he was able to converse with the Bedouin, and replied to the questions which were put to him.

The captains then endeavoured to come to an understanding with the natives. They landed the Bedouin with one of the Moorish women they had captured, charging them to go and invite the natives to come and negotiate with them for the ransom of the prisoners, or to treat for the exchange of merchandise.

[1] This harbour is marked in the map of Africa in the Portuguese atlas in the Bibliothèque Nationale, Paris, and in another Portuguese map on parchment in the same collection, and also of the sixteenth century. The name is seen on the hither side of Cape Blanco.

[2] A Moor from the North of Africa, whom Nuno Tristão had brought with him, hoping that he would be able to understand the natives of the West Coast.

[3] *Vide* RITTER, *Geog. comp.*, vol. iii, 366. *Azenagha*. This author states that they speak Berber.

[4] Sahara. The inhabitants were known as *Saharacin*, "sons of the desert."

After the lapse of two days there came down to the shore some hundred and fifty Moors on foot and thirty-five riders on horses and camels, and they brought the Bedouin with them. And albeit their aspect was that of a people barbarous and bestial, they were not wanting in cunning, of which they endeavoured to make use in deceiving their enemies. For only three showed themselves, and the others remained hidden, to fall upon our men, whom they hoped to see disembark; which they very well might have done, their numbers being so great, if our men had been less prudent.

But seeing that those who came toward them in the ships' boats, not having perceived the Bedouin, turned sharply about, the Moors immediately betrayed their ruse, all suddenly springing up at the mouth of the river, casting stones and manifesting their ill-will; and they then showed the Bedouin, bound with cords, as a captive, and the same told our men that they should beware of these people, since they had come only to do them injury.

Thereupon our men returned to their ships, where they made division of their captives by lot; and the Moors went off, carrying the Bedouin with them.

Antão Gonçalves, whose ship was already laden in accordance with the Infante's orders, returned to Portugal, and Nuno Tristão continued his voyage along the coast, as he was bound to do in order to accomplish his mission. Howbeit, after the departure of Antão Gonçalves, his caravel being in need of repair, he caused it to be drawn up ashore, where it was cleaned and repaired while waiting for the tide, as though he had been in Lisbon harbour, a feat whose boldness provoked the admiration of his men. Then, continuing their voyage, they went beyond Porto da Galé until they came to a cape which they named Cabo Branco,[1] where they landed in the hope of making some capture; but although they found the imprints of men's feet, and also nets, they did not undertake to go farther, and resolved to return to Portugal, since they could not do there anything more than they had already done.

. . .

. . . Although the language of these first captives could not be understood by any of the other Moors who were in the kingdom, free or prisoner, that which the African knight brought by Antão Gonçalves was able to say was nevertheless enough to give the Infante intelligence of a great measure of the affairs of that region which he inhabited.

And Dom Henrique, considering that armed vessels carrying his men must needs often go thither—for it would be necessary to war against the Infidels there— immediately made ready to send an embassy to the Holy Father to ask him to share with him the treasures of the Holy Church, in order that those who might lose their lives in these conquests should have their souls saved[2] . . .

. . .

[1] Cape Blanco.

[2] The Pope (Martin V) conceded what was asked of him. Pope Nicolas V despatched another Bull, dated January 8, 1450, conceding to King Dom Affonso V all the territories which the Infante Dom Henrique had discovered. On January 8, 1454, the same Pope confirmed and conceded by another Bull, to King Dom Affonso V and the Infante Dom Henrique, and all the Kings of Portugal their successors, all the conquests made in Africa, from Cape Bojador and the Cabo de Nao to the whole of Guinea, with all its southern coast. On March 13, 1455,

And the Infante Dom Pedro, who was at this time regent of the kingdom during the minority of the King, granted to his brother Dom Henrique the fifth part of all that belonged to the King (as the outcome of these African discoveries); and this by reason of the great expenditure made by Dom Henrique for this purpose. And as these things had been sought and found by the Infante with great travail and expense, no one might go thither in future without his permission or express order.

· · ·

The Moorish knight taken on the last expedition, desiring to obtain his freedom, declared to Antão Gonçalves that in his country they would give five or six negroes for his ransom. He said also that among the other captives were two young Moors whose ransom would yield as much as his own.

As the Infante already knew all that the Moorish knight and the two young Moors could tell him of the African countries known to them, he resolved to send Antão Gonçalves with them to undertake their ransom, in the hope that he might learn more from the negroes obtained in exchange.

A gentleman of the Court of the Emperor of Almain, Frederick III, being at this time in Lisbon, and desirous of distinguishing himself by perilous adventures, and above all of seeing a great storm at sea, the Infante permitted him to sail with Antão Gonçalves. They ran into a storm so terrible that they

Calixtus III ordained, by another Bull, that the parts of West Africa discovered and acquired by Portugal, as well as all territories discovered in future, should belong only to the Kings of Portugal; and he confirmed the Bulls of Martin V and Nicolas V.

were like to lose their lives in it. Nevertheless, having returned to Portugal they re-embarked and began their voyage anew.

The Moorish knight was set ashore near the Rio do Ouro that he might go in quest of his ransom, Antão Gonçalves confiding in his word as a gentleman. He had been very well treated, and he was well clad. Nevertheless, he was seen no more.

But the Moors came to ransom the two young men, and gave in exchange for these two youths ten negroes, men and women of different countries, of whom several understood the Moorish tongue. And over and above these negroes Antão Gonçalves received a little gold dust,[1] a buckler, and many ostriches' eggs.

To go by what these Moors related, there were in this place merchants who trafficked in gold. This gold came from the country of the negroes called Ouangara.[2]

. . .

. . . In this fashion the knowledge of these matters was little by little increased, and men became accustomed to engage in voyages, some in service, others for honour, and others in the hope of profit, albeit all these came to one and the same thing, inasmuch

---

[1] The name of *Rio de Ouro* was given to this gulf because it was thence that the Portuguese first brought home gold. The Rio do Ouro (River of Gold) is not a river, but an arm of the sea, which runs some fifteen miles inland.

[2] *Vide* EDRISI and IBN-EL-OUARDI, *Notices et extrait des manuscrits de la Bibliothèque du Roi.* This gold had been brought from the interior, by caravans, from the earliest historic times. Under the Empire of the Khalifs this trade from the interior of Africa extended not only to the western shores of the Continent but also to Spain. The caravans traversed the valleys and plains of Suz, Darah, and Tafilet, in the south of Morocco. (*Vide* GEO. NUBIENSIS, 1613, pp. 7, 11, 12; and HARTMANN's *Edrisi*, pp. 25, 49, 133, 134.)

as serving they increased their honour and had their reward.

In the year of Christ 1443 the Infante caused another caravel to be armed, in which he sent out this noble knight Nuno Tristão with certain others, and above all persons of his household; and pursuing their voyage, they came to Cape Blanco. And wishing to go farther, they sailed yet another twenty-five leagues and found a little island, whose name they learned afterwards: Isle of Geta.[1]

They saw twenty-five small boats leaving the island, full of persons who were quite naked, not because of the water, but because such was their ancient custom. Their bodies were in the boats, but their legs were in the water, and they made use of them as they were oars. And in each boat there were three or four men.

Our men having never beheld such a thing, and regarding them from afar, believed that they were birds, although their size was too great; but marvels yet more astonishing were told of these parts. However, so soon as they drew near and saw what was in truth before them their hearts were filled with joy, and this above all because they understood that they could capture them with ease.

But they could not take many of them because of

[1] This is Arguin Island. The discovery and possession of this island were of great importance for the Portuguese. It facilitated their means of obtaining information and establishing commercial relations with the negro states situated on the banks of the Senegal and Gambia Rivers. The Infante had a fortress built there, work upon which was begun in 1448. He maintained a garrison there, and a factory, and three vessels found harbourage. The Portuguese retained possession of the island until 1638. At that date the Dutch took the factory and the fortress. The island has belonged successively to the English, the Dutch, and the French, who have retained possession of it.

the littleness of their barge, which had gone from the caravel to encounter these boats; for it would not hold more than fourteen captives, being already laden with seven of our own men.

They wished to return thither, but that availed them nothing, for the terror was so great among the enemies that they fled in great haste, and some died and the rest escaped. . . . But landing on the island, they took yet other fourteen Moors.[1]

Near this island they discovered another where there were royal herons in infinite number,[2] which it seems assemble there to make their nests; and many other birds, of which they secured great store.

And Nuno Tristão returned with his captives, more joyous than the first time because the take was greater, and also because he was alone and had no need to share it.

[1] The Portuguese gave the name of Moor to all Infidels.
[2] This island was called *Ilha das Garcas*. It is so marked in the old maps. In Gastaldi's map, published in Venice in 1564, which comprises the geographical data of the Portuguese maps, it is shown as the *Ile* or *Banc des Garces*.

CHAPTER IV

*How Lançarote asked leave of the Infante to set out
with other captains and a number of vessels to take his
chance in Africa, and what was the outcome of this
expedition*

. . .

THE men of the *plebs*, according to the saying of
Titus Livius, criticize and speak ill of great feats,
above all in their beginnings. And this, it seems to
me, must be because they cannot comprehend the
ends envisaged; in considering great matters those
whose minds are narrow believe them greater than
they are, and because their spirits cannot rise to their
greatness they doubt their achievement.

I saw an example of this during the achievements
of the Infante Dom Henrique, for when he began to
populate the isles the people did nothing but murmur
among themselves, as though it were being done at
their cost. They were full of misgivings, and were
never done with babbling of it, presenting the facts
in such a manner that in the end no one could believe
in a good outcome.

But when the isles were populated in such a fashion
that people profited by the land, and when the fruits
of this labour began to reach the kingdom in great
plenty, those who had mistrusted the venture held
their peace, and under their breath they praised what
they had at first publicly dispraised.

The same thing befell at the beginning of these
discoveries and conquests in Africa; for during the

first years, perceiving the labours of the Infante's shipyards, and the ships that went forth, and all the disbursements of this prince, the people set aside their own affairs and busied themselves with censuring these matters of which they knew so little; and the longer the results tarried, the sharper was their dispraise. And what was worse, not only did the common people speak thus, but also the great, who babbled of these things almost as though in mockery, saying that of all these labours and all these disbursements there would never be any profit.

But when they saw the first company of Moors arrive, and then the second, they began to doubt their judgment. They understood how far they had deceived themselves when Nuno Tristão disembarked with the third company of captives, taken in so short a time and with so little labour. Then they confessed their error, understanding their foolishness in having spoken concerning matters they did not comprehend; they changed their censure for public praise, declaring that the Infante was a second Alexander. And envy began to gnaw at them as they saw the houses of others filled with servants, and their possessions increased; and considering all these things, they debated them among themselves.

Since his return from Tangier the Infante was almost always in the province of Algarve, by reason of the city which he was engaged in building, and the captives and other booties which were brought back from the conquest were landed at Lagos. The people of Lagos were therefore the first to ask the Infante for leave to go to the countries whence these Moors were brought; for no ship could go thither without the special permission of the Infante, in accordance with the charter which the King had granted him, and in which he also gave the Infante for himself the fifth part of that which fell due to him of all booty, as you already know.

The first who undertook to ask for this permission was Lançarote, a squire, reared from childhood in the household of the Infante, who was already married, and had the charge of King's treasurer in this city of Lagos. Because he was a discreet and thoughtful man he understood the progress of these matters and the profit which he could derive from them, if so be God granted him a fortunate voyage.

He spoke to certain of his friends, persuading them to accompany him in this enterprise, which was not a hard thing for him, since he was greatly esteemed in the city, and because the men of Lagos were valiant men, desirous of winning distinction, above all in maritime undertakings, for Lagos lies hard by the shore, and they were all more habituated to the things of the sea than to those of the dry land.

Lançarote thus got together six caravels well equipped, and he spoke to the Infante to obtain his permission, saying that he asked it in order to serve him, and also for his own honour and profit; and he told him who were the men who accompanied him, and the number of the caravels and their armament. The Infante was well content therewith, and straightway caused banners to be made with the cross of the Order of Christ, commanding that each caravel should have its banner . . .

. . .

The first captain and the chief, as we have already

declared, was Lançarote, and the second Gil Eannes, he who first passed beyond Cape Bojador; and Estevão Affonso, a nobleman who was afterwards to die in the Canary Isles; and Rodrigo Alvares, and João Dias, shipwright, and João Bernardes; and they were all well provided and prepared for this voyage.

They came to the Isle of Herons on the eve of Corpus Christi, and there they lay some time, by reason chiefly of the multitude of birds which they found there, for it was the season of nesting. And then they held council as to what they were about to do, and Lançarote set forth his reasons as follows:

"Lords and friends! We have left our country to serve God and the Infante our lord, and he must needs look for great services from us, as much by reason of the rearing which he gave to some among us as by reason of the men we are; thereto it would be a shame to us to do no better than all the others who have hitherto come to these parts; it would be a truly shameful thing should so many ships together return to Portugal without a very great prize. The Infante has learned from some of these Moors taken to Portugal by Nuno Tristão that in the island of Naar[1] not far from here there is a population of nigh on two hundred souls. It seems to me, then, that Martin Vicente and Gil Vasques, who have already been near this island and know where it lies, should go thither in our ships' boats, taking only the men needed to row. And if they can find the island they should return very quickly along the coast to meet us, since for our part, God permitting, we shall make sail

---

[1] This island is shown near the coast of Arguin on the map of Africa in the Portuguese atlas in the Bibliothèque Nationale, Paris.

very early in the morning, so that on meeting them we shall be so near that we can hear their news, take counsel as to what is proper to be done, and forthwith do it."

Lançarote, as I have said, was a discreet and thoughtful man, whom all the others had in respect; therefore they did not discuss his reasons, which all approved.

The two captains appointed made ready to set out; they took five boats with thirty men; that is, in each boat six men; and they left the island where they lay about the hour of sunset.

They rowed all that night, and towards the break of day they came near to the isle which they were seeking. And as they recognized it by the indications which the Moors had given them, they rowed along the shore. In the morning they perceived a population of Moors near the sea, and there all the inhabitants of the island were gathered together. They then stayed their way and came together to resolve what they would now do.

· · ·

If they attacked, they would disobey the orders of Lançarote; but if they returned without essaying to capture these natives, they would run a great risk of losing them, for as the day was already dawning they would be discovered by the Moors, who would flee and warn the people of the other islands, which were all very near the coast. And Martin Affonso, who was of opinion that they should attack, set forth his reasons, and concluded as follows:

· · ·

". . . And as to the order which we have from our captain, if God aids us, and if we can perform some goodly exploit, which is what I hope, we could not be blamed therefor, and this for two reasons: the first, because if we do not fight we are sure that our voyage will be wasted, and we shall not be able to satisfy the desires of our lord the Infante; the second is that even if we have the order to turn about, we have not been ordered not to fight. Now, battle seems to me reasonable, for we are on our side thirty men, and the Moors, according to what you have heard, are seventy or eighty in all, of whom some fifty or sixty will be warriors. If you are agreed, let us not tarry, for the day is drawing on, and the least delay will render fruitless our presence and our council."

And as he ended this speech they looked in the direction of the tribe, and saw that the Moors, with their women and children, were issuing in haste from their dwellings, for they had seen them. And our men, crying "Santiago! San Jorge! Portugal!" fell upon them, killing and capturing as many as they could.

Then you might see mothers abandoning their children and husbands abandoning their wives, each thinking only to flee as speedily as might be. And some drowned themselves in the sea, others sought refuge in their huts, others hid their children under the mud, thinking that thus they might conceal them from the eyes of the enemy, and that they could come to seek them later. And at length Our Lord God, Who rewardeth all that is well done, ordained that in return for the work of this day done by our men in His service they should have the victory over their enemies and the reward of their fatigues and disbursements, in the taking of one hundred and sixty-five captives, men, women, and children, without reckoning those that died or that killed themselves.

When the battle was ended they said their prayers to thank God for having thus vouchsafed to give them the victory. And having embarked their captives in the boats, and leaving others on shore securely bound —for the boats were small and could not contain so many people—they sent one of their men along the coast as far as he could go, essaying to see if the caravels were coming to meet them. And he, having marched a good league, at length perceived the caravels, for Lançarote, in accordance with his word, had set forth at dawn. This man affixed a white cloak to the end of his lance and began to make signals to the caravels, which, having seen him, came towards him. And those aboard the caravels having noted a sort of channel by which their boats could enter the island, launched one into the water and landed in quest of news. He who was awaiting them related what had passed, and required them to accompany him, and to help him to bring off the captives, who had been left on shore under the guard of six men; for the other boats were already on their way along the coast with the captive Moors.

When Lançarote with his squires and others who were with him heard such news, and understood what mighty aid God had given these men, few as they were, who had come to this island, and when they considered the noble feats which they had accomplished, they gave thanks to God and were right joyful, praising Lord God in that He had thus aided this little band of Christians.

.   .   .

. . . Lançarote did not forget to question the captive Moors, through his interpreter, concerning such things as he wished to know; in what place he was, and what season; and he learned that there were near by other inhabited islands where he and his men might without too great fatigue make good captures. And he having assembled the council, they were agreed to set forth without delay in quest of these islands.   . . .

On the following day, which was a Friday, they made ready their boats, lading them with provisions enough for two days, for they did not intend to remain longer away from the caravels. And in the boats there were thirty men, that is to say, Lançarote and the other captains of the caravels, and with them the squires and other men. And they took with them also two of the captive Moors, for these had told them that in the Isle of Tider, which lay at a distance of five leagues, there was a tribe of one hundred and fifty Moors . . .

When they came to it they found the village deserted, for the inhabitants had fled. They resolved to divide themselves into two companies, of which one would remain with the boats to guard them, and, in case of need, would succour the others, while the second company went on foot toward another village, guided by one of the captives.

. . . Lançarote, with fourteen or fifteen men, set forth guided by the Moor. And when they were already half a league from the place where the others were remaining they saw nine Moors, men and women, with ten or twelve asses laden with turtles, and they were crossing over to the Isle of Tider,[1] which lay a league distant. When the tide was low it was possible thus to pass on foot from the one island to the other.

Our men ran in upon them and took them all, excepting one who contrived to flee, and who went to warn those that were in the village . . .

So that when they came to the village they found no one there, and saw the natives on a sandbank, to which they had fled for refuge on their rafts, but at which our men could not come save by swimming, since the sea was not deep enough to enable the boats to pass. Accordingly they did not go thither, but on passing again through the village they found hidden seven or eight women, whom they took with them.

· · ·

Having returned to their boats, they rested during the night, after they had agreed concerning what they should do on the morrow. And they resolved to go once again to this village about dawn, saying that the natives, having seen them go, might have returned to their houses, thinking themselves now in safety.

· · ·

. . . It was yet night when they set forth, steering their boats along the coast; and at dawn they disembarked and ran to the village, but they found no one there, for the Moors, although they had returned to the village on the previous evening after their departure, would by no means pass the night there. They had encamped a quarter of a league from the

---

[1] Isle of Tider. This island, and also the Isle of Naar and the Isle of Herons, are shown in the old maps near the Arguin coast. In the Isolaris of Bordone (1533), in which these islands are shown, they are all three described as the Isles of the Herons; and the same in Gastaldi's and other maps.

village, at a part of the coast where they could readily reach Tider.

When the Christians saw that the Moors were no longer in the village they returned to their boats, and rowed along that part of the coast which looks upon Tider; and they sent fifteen men overland with orders to seek some place where the Moors might have taken refuge, or signs of their passage. And as they were on the way they perceived the Moors, who were fleeing as fast as they could, for they had seen our men; who disembarked in haste and pursued them. They could not come at the men, but they seized some seventeen or eighteen women and children, for these could not run so fast. One of the boats, in which was João Bernardes, and which was one of the smallest, continued to follow the shore; those who were in this boat saw a score of rafts which were making for Tider, carrying Moors, men and women, great and small, and each raft contained four to five persons.

This caused them at first much joy; but soon this joy was transformed into grief. The joy came of finding so fair an occasion of honour and profit; but great grief seized upon them on perceiving how small was their boat, which could hold but a few persons. And with oars so few they nevertheless went their way as swiftly as they might, until they found themselves surrounded by rafts; and moved by pity, albeit these rafts were filled with Infidels, they killed only a very few. However, it must be believed that many Moors who, seized with fear, abandoned the rafts, perished in the sea. And the Christians thus passing amidst the rafts chose above all the children, in order to carry off more of them in their boat; of them they took fourteen. On numbering the Moors whom they took during these two days, apart from a few who died, there were forty-eight.

With this good booty, and rendering thanks to God for having thus guided and aided them, and for having given them the victory over the enemies of the faith, and more than ever desirous of labouring well to serve God, they took to their boats again and returned toward the caravels, which lay at a distance of five leagues. And on reaching them they took a little rest, for they had great need of the same.

But this rest was not long, for towards evening they assembled in council to decide what they would now do, wishing to make the most profitable use of their time while fortune favoured them.

Gil Eannes spoke at length, counselling them to go to the Isle of Tider, which lay at no great distance, and on which the captive Moors declared there was a considerable population. And if these natives were too many for them to fight, they might perchance learn something as to their numbers in order to carry the news to the Infante.

All were in agreement with Gil Eannes, and on the morrow, at break of day, the boats set out anew, carrying thirty men.

. . .

. . . They came to Tider at noon. Twenty men landed, and ten remained in the boats. The twenty marched inland about half a league, looking well in all directions in the hope of discovering some inhabitants in their houses; and on climbing a little hill they saw two Moors who were coming towards them, but who did not perceive them, or took them to be inhabitants of the island. The Christians fell upon them and overcame them. And farther on they saw ten Moors who were driving fifteen or twenty asses laden with fish; and they attacked them. The Moors essayed to defend themselves, but in vain; soon they fled in all directions and were all taken. And then two of our men went forward a little farther in the hope of discovering other Moors, and they saw many, who, having seen them, ran at them. The two Portuguese fled toward their companions who had remained with the prisoners, and told them what had passed, bidding them escape as quickly as possible, for a multitude of Moors was coming down upon them.

They accordingly set out for the boats, running, but carrying with them all their prisoners; and the Moors pursued them as swiftly as they were able.

It was the will of God—Who, in anguish and peril, comes to the aid of those who labour in His service— that the Christians should reach the shore before the arrival of the Moors; nevertheless, before they had time to jump into their boats the Moors were already upon them, and all were fighting in a great mellay. It was with enormous effort and difficulty that the Christians contrived to get into their boats. In this encounter all showed themselves so valiant and skilful, and gave such proof of the strength and ardour of their courage, that one could not say that one was more valiant than another. And Lançarote and a squire of the Infante who was called Martin Vaz were the last to be taken into the boats.

The Moors were some three hundred warriors, who gave good proof of their will to defend their country.

Many of them were wounded by the Christians, and of these it pleased God that none were grievously hurt. And so soon as they were in their boats, with all their prisoners, they made toward the caravels; and it was already night.

.   .   .

They resolved to sail on the morrow for Cape Blanco, where after two days they arrived, and there they landed. And having encountered some natives, they fought them and made fourteen prisoners. Marching then towards the interior of the island, they discovered a village, but the inhabitants having had intelligence of their approach had fled; one young girl only had remained, and her they took with them. Then, having rejoined the caravels, they set sail for Portugal.

.   .   .

The caravels arrived in Lagos, whence they had set out, having made a good voyage, for fortune was no less favourable to them in the fair weather which she accorded them than she had been in the capture of their booty. And the news reached the Infante at the moment when he arrived in Lagos, having been absent some days from this city.

You know how people are ever anxious to hear the news; some came down to the shore; others leaped into the boats which they found moored along the beach, and went to welcome their kinsfolk and friends; so that the good news of the success of this voyage was quickly noised about, by which everyone was overjoyed.

And this day the captains did no more than go to kiss the hand of the prince their seigneur, declaring to him briefly what they had performed; and they

then returned to their own homes, giving themselves
wholly to the joy of having returned to their own
country and their own households, where you may
conceive what would be their joy in being restored
to their wives and children.

On the morrow Lançarote—who was that one
among the captains who had more especially been
given the command of this expedition—said to the
Infante: "Lord, you know that the fifth part of these
Moors belongs to you, as of all other things brought
by us from these countries to which you sent us in
God's service and your own. And behold: these
Moors, by reason of the long months which we have
spent at sea, and the grief which, as you may well
conceive, they have in their hearts—finding themselves
so far from their native land, and captives, and
knowing nought of what is to befall them; and further,
by reason of their lack of habituation to sea-going—
are very sick and ill-disposed. It seems to me then
that to-morrow morning you should cause them to
be landed outside the city gate; and that there they
should be divided into five groups, according to
custom, and that of these five portions you should
come to choose that which may best please you."

The Infante having said that this would be pleasing
to him, on the morrow, very early, Lançarote ordered
the boatswains to land the captives and lead them to
this place, dividing them into five groups or parties
as was agreed. But before all else they took the best
of these Moors as an offering to the Church of the
city; and to St. Vincent of the Cape they sent a little
boy chosen from among the captives, who afterwards
became a religious of the order of St. Francis, having

always lived as a Catholic Christian, and having knowledge or sentiment of no other religion, but only this, holy and veritable, to which all we Christians look for our salvation.

And the number of the Moors of this capture was two hundred and thirty-five.

. . .

Oh, Thou Heavenly Father, Who with Thy mighty hand, without debasing Thy Divine essence, dost govern the infinite population of Thy holy city . . . I implore Thee: let my tears trouble not my conscience, for it is not the law of the Infidels, but their quality of human beings, that constrains me to weep for pity in the face of their sufferings. And if the animals, the brute creation, with their beast-like sentiments, by a natural instinct know the grief of their kind, how wouldst Thou that my human nature should not be troubled when I have thus before my eyes this miserable cohort, and remember that they are of the generation of the sons of Adam!

On the morrow, the eighth day of the month of August, in the morning, very early by reason of the heat, the sailors began to fill their boats, taking the captives from the caravels to lead them where they had been commanded. And when they were all assembled in this field it was truly a thing astonishing to behold; for among them there were some wellnigh white, who were handsome and well made in body; others were black as Ethiopians, and so uncomely, as well in countenance as in body, that those who were guarding them thought they beheld the creatures of the lower hemisphere.

But what heart, even the hardest, would not be

moved by a sentiment of pity on seeing such a flock;
for some held their heads bowed down, and their
faces were bathed with tears; others were groaning
grievously, lifting their eyes to the heavens, fixing
them upon the heights, and raising an outcry as
though imploring the Father of Nature to succour
them; others beat upon their faces with their hands
and cast themselves at length upon the ground; others
raised their lamentations in the manner of a chant,
according to the custom of their country; and although
the words uttered in their language could not be
understood by us, it was plain that they were consonant
with the degree of their grief.

Then, as though the more to increase their suffering,
came those who were commanded to make the
division; and they began to part them one from
another, in order to form companies, in such manner
that each should be of equal value; and for this it
was necessary to separate children from their parents,
and women from their husbands, and brothers from
brothers. There was no law in respect of kinship
or affection; each had perforce to go whither fate
drove him.

Oh! mighty Fortune who turnest thy wheel this
way or that, ordering the things of this world according
to thy good pleasure! Thou hast not even deigned to
set before the eyes of these unhappy people the least
knowledge of things to come, from which they might
have drawn some consolation in the midst of their
great sorrow! And you others, who are busying
yourselves with this division, look with pity upon so
much misery, and consider how they cling one to
another, in such wise that you can hardly part them!

Who, without much travail, could have made such a division? So soon as they had been led to their place the sons, seeing themselves removed from their parents, ran hastily towards them; the mothers clasped their children in their arms, and holding them, cast themselves upon the ground, covering them with their bodies, without heeding the blows which they were given!

And thus, with much difficulty, they were at length divided. Apart from this labour, the field was full of people as well from the city as from the villages and the country round about; leaving for this day the labours that nourished them, they had come for no other purpose than to behold this new thing. And on considering these things, some weeping, others speaking and moving to and fro, they created such a disorder and such a din that those who had to make the division were bewildered thereby.

The Infante was there upon a great horse, in the midst of his people; he parcelled out his share like a man who was by no means eager to possess great treasures; since of the forty souls who fell to him he forthwith made presents, because his wealth was only in his will, and he had no other pleasure than in thinking that these lost souls would now be saved.

His thought was not vain, for, as we have said, so soon as the Moors comprehended our language without difficulty they became Christians; and I who am writing this history have seen in the city of Lagos boys and girls, the children and grandchildren of those Moors, born in our country, as good and true Christians as though they had been descended, since

the commencement of Christ's law, from those who
were the first to be baptized . . .

. . . . .

. . . The tears of the captives were abundant,
above all after the parcelling out which parted them,
each being taken off separately; and some of those
to whom they belonged sold them, and thus they
were removed to other regions of the country, the
father remaining in Lagos, the mother going to
Lisbon, and the children to some other place, which
doubled their grief; others were more fortunate, for
fate had left them together, and the proverb says:
Solatio est miseris socios habere pena. Howbeit, they
became acquainted with the country, where they
found abundance and were well treated; for finding
that they were not hardened in their beliefs, like the
other Moors,[1] and seeing that they embraced the law
of Christ without difficulty, people made no difference
between them and their free servants, native to the
country. And as for those whom they acquired in
their youth, they even had them taught mechanical
trades; to those whom they saw disposed to gain their
livelihood they gave their liberty, married them to
women of the country, and gave them property; as
though they had received them at the desire of their
relatives, and as though they owed them a reward
for their good service.

Some of the honest widows who bought these
captives adopted them as daughters; others made
them heirs of their wealth, so that afterwards they
made good marriages and became wholly free.

I never saw chains on any of these captives, as I

[1] Arab captives from North Africa.

have seen upon others; there was hardly one but became a Christian and was treated with much kindness. I have been invited by their masters to witness their baptism and marriage; and I have seen that these sacraments were administered with as much solemnity as though they had been the children or kinsfolk of their masters.

Thus, having left the country in which they were dwelling to the perdition of their souls and bodies, they had now all things to the contrary. I say perdition of their souls, because they were pagans without the light or flame of the holy faith; and of their bodies, because they lived like beasts, without any of the customs of rational creatures, since they did not even know what were bread and wine, nor garments of cloth, nor life in the shelter of a house; and worse still was their ignorance, which deprived them of all knowledge of good, and permitted them only a life of brutish idleness. And so soon as they came to our country and were given artificial foods, and raiment for their bodies, their bellies began to swell, and they fell sick, until they had adapted themselves to the nature of this country; and some were of such complexion that they could not support them, and died, but they died Christians.

There were in these people four things which made them very different from the other Moorish captives in the realm: the first, that being in this country they did not seek to escape, and after some little time they even forgot their country, once they had comprehended the advantages of this; the second, that they were very loyal and obedient, and bore no malice; the third, that they were not so inclined to lewdness as the others; and the fourth, immediately they were clad they were taken with the taste for baubles and gaudy colours; and this in such a degree that they would gather up the rags of coloured garments which were of no more service to the people of the country, and would sew them upon their costumes, so making them, to their thinking, more comely, and having as much joy of them as if they had been very fine things.

And, which was best of all, they followed with a willing heart—as I have said—the path of faith, in which, once having entered upon it, they became truly believers, making it the purpose of their lives.

See now what must surely be the reward of the Infante before the presence of the Lord God for having thus saved not these souls alone but many and many more, as you shall see by the continuation of this history!

When the parcelling out was ended the captains of the other caravels went to find the Infante, as did also some other servants of his household, and they said to him: "Lord! Since you know the great labour that Lançarote, your servant, has undergone in order to bring this enterprise to a good end, and what effort and goodwill he has put forth, which have been the cause of the victory that God has given you; and also because he is descended of a good lineage, we beg you to do us the favour of making him knight with your own hand, since you see that he deserves it in every fashion. And even if he did not so well deserve it," said the captains, "it seems to us that we should be offended—since he is our captain, and since he has done so good a work before our eyes—if he did not receive as reward some honour greater than those which he already has, being valiant and your servant, as we have already said."

The Infante replied that their words pleased him greatly, and that he thanked them for having thus spoken, for in this manner they set a good example.

And without further delay he made Lançarote knight, loading him with benefits according to his merits and his valour. And he likewise granted benefits to all the other captains, so that over and above the gain they had of their captures they had others which rewarded them right well for all their fatigues.

CHAPTER V

*Voyage and death of Gonçalo de Sintra. How João
Fernandes was left alone in the land of Africa in order
to give intelligence thereof to the Infante. How Diniz
Dias was the first to see the land of the Negroes (Guinea).
Of the first captives disembarked at Lisbon. Of the
voyage of Gonçalo Pacheco and the death of the seven
Portuguese. Of the voyage of Lançarote with his fleet of
fourteen caravels and of the other twelve caravels which
sailed with him; their discoveries and adventures*

YOU must know that this Gonçalo de Sintra of
whom we shall speak was a squire reared from
childhood in the household of the Infante . . . and
because he was a man of goodly stature and a great
heart the Infante had shown him much favour,
entrusting him always with honourable and important
missions.

Some little while after the return of Lançarote the
Infante caused to be equipped a caravel, in which he
sent Gonçalo de Sintra as captain, recommending
him before his departure to go directly to Guinea,
and in no event to do anything else.

Gonçalo de Sintra, pursuing his voyage, came to
Cape Blanco, and—see how men are carried away
by their desire of renown!—he said to his companions that he was fain to go to the Arguin Isles
which were near this place, since it seemed to him
that without great danger they could take some
prisoners . . .

The expedition was ill-fated, and Gonçalo de

Sintra came by his death, as did also seven of his companions.[1]

. . .

. . . This year [1445] the Infante sent Antão Gonçalves, that noble knight of whom we have already spoken, in a caravel; and Gomes Pires, a shipmaster in the King's service, in another. This caravel was sent forth by the Infante Dom Pedro, who at this time was governing the realm in the King's name. And there was also one other caravel whose captain was a certain Diogo Affonso, a servant of the Infante Dom Henrique. The purpose of their voyage was if might be to come to an understanding with the Moors of these regions, in order that they might make arrangement for the exchange of merchandise.

. . .

But their efforts were fruitless, and they returned from their voyage bringing with them only one aged Moor . . .

. . . who, of his own free will, desired to go and see the Infante, who received him right well, giving him many presents and sending him back in freedom to his country.

But I am less astonished by the coming of this negro than by this: a squire who went with Antão Gonçalves, and who was called João Fernandes, of his own will desired to remain in this land of Africa, merely to gain knowledge of it that he might give intelligence thereof to the Infante when he should

---

[1] This happened in the year 1445. The place is situated thirty-five miles to the south of the Rio do Ouro: and since the end of the fifteenth century it has been marked on manuscript and printed maps as the Gulf of Gonçalo de Sintra.

find occasion to return to his own country. And of what came to pass in respect of this squire and his goodwill I shall say somewhat later.

• • •

To apprise you how matters passed we shall here declare how Nuno Tristão, of whom we have already spoken on divers occasions in the course of this history, was the first to behold the *Land of the Negroes*.

The Infante had sent him in a caravel to these countries. He sailed to the isles which he had already visited,[1] now become desert, for the inhabitants, dreading the evil which had come upon them, had departed for the time being to other islands, of which they believed that their enemies had as yet no knowledge.

Nuno Tristão and his companions, seeing that they could not take captives on these islands, resolved to go farther.

. . . And they sailed beyond these regions, and came to another, very different; for the first was sandy and barren, without trees, like a land deprived of water; and in the other three were very many palms and other trees, green and very fair, and all the fields looked to be fertile in that country.[2]

Azurara relates that the natives came down to the shore as though wishing to communicate with the men of the caravel; but the sea being rough the boats

---

[1] The Heron Islands in the great Arguin bank.

[2] Nuno Tristão, having recognized the Arguin Isles, discovered along the coast, to the southward, Ilha Branca, Rio de S. João, Golfo de Santa Anna, Montas, Praias, Furna, Costa d'Arca, Resgate and *Palmar*, this latter being surely the place where the author states that he saw *very many palms*.

could not make a landing, and the caravel could not remain at anchor, but was obliged to sail on.

Nuno Tristão landed near the place where Lançarote had made his capture, and he took captive a score of Moors.

The scrupulous conscience of the chronicler is manifested by the manner in which he concludes this chapter:

. . . they took only twenty-one, but we do not find in any writing whether among these twenty-one there were women or children, nor yet how many men accompanied Nuno Tristão, nor if there was any fighting before the capture; and we cannot know, for Nuno Tristão was already dead when the King Dom Affonso commanded me to write this history. And for these reasons we shall leave the recital thus without further explanations . . .

There was in Lisbon a noble squire—who had been a servant of the King Dom João, grandfather of King Dom Affonso and father of the virtuous Infante Dom Henrique—who was called Diniz Dias.[1] Having heard what was related of these new countries, and how the caravels had already gone so far from our shore, he sought the Infante Dom Henrique and entreated him to send him into these lands of Africa, for having been reared by the King his father, being a servant of his household, and still of an age and a heart to do good service, he was unwilling to permit himself to grow soft in the well-being of repose; for he was a man desirous of seeing new things and of putting his strength to the proof; although he had the means to dwell in peace in this city [of Lisbon], which was one of the noblest in the Spains, and was in enjoyment

[1] Or Diniz Fernandes.

of profitable offices which had been awarded him for good services.

The Infante thanked Diniz Dias for his goodwill, and straightway caused a caravel to be armed in order to satisfy his desire. Diniz Dias, having set forth with his ship's company, was not willing to stop until he had passed the country of the Moors and come in sight of the *Land of the Negroes* which is called Guinea. And as in the course of this history we have sometimes given the name of Guinea to that other country to which the first navigators went, we would say that this region is not the same, for there is a great difference between the two, and they are very far apart one from the other, as we shall explain later, when the occasion presents itself.

And as they continued their voyage along this sea the natives who were on the shore perceived the caravel, at which they were filled with amazement. Never, assuredly, had they seen or heard tell of such marvel; these believed that the caravel was a fish, and those a phantom; others again said that it might be a bird. And four of them were so hardy as to put out to sea so as to look more closely at the cause of their astonishment. They embarked in a little canoe fashioned from a hollow tree-trunk. . . . The natives came towards the caravel, and those on board could not resist the temptation to appear on the deck; and when the negroes saw these men they fled as swiftly as they might. And although the caravel pursued them, since the wind was very faint, the negroes contrived to escape.

Our navigators continued on their course, and a little farther on they perceived other native canoes, which, seeing that our sailors were men, being astonished by such a novelty, and seized with dread, sought to escape; but because the occasion was more favourable than the first, the Portuguese were able to take four of these negroes; the first who in their own country were captured by white men. There is no chronicle or history that declares the contrary. This was a great honour for our prince, whose power was so great as to send men thus far from our kingdom and make captives among people so near to the land of Egypt.[1]

Diniz Dias ought to share this honour, since he was the first who, by order of the Infante, made captives of Moors in this country; and still pursuing his voyage, he rounded a great cape to which he gave the name *Cape Verde*. And he says that there were many people there, but we have not found in writing in what manner the caravel encountered these people; whether they saw them on shore or in their boats, fishing. In any event, they made no more captures in the course of this voyage; but they disembarked on an island, where they found many goats and birds, of which they made large provision; and also they found many things that were wholly different from those of our country, as we shall afterwards relate.

Although the capture was not so great as those that had been made previously, the Infante considered it of great import, because it came from this country (hitherto unknown), and for that reason he granted great benefits to Diniz Dias and his men . . .

[1] Error of the systematic geography of the ancients, still current at this period.

Azurara then recounts the voyage of Antão Gonçalves, Garcia Homem, and Diogo Affonso, who set forth on three caravels at the request of the first-named, meaning to essay the recovery of that squire João Fernandes who had remained of his own will in these unknown regions in order to bring back from them intelligence for the Infante. The first part of this voyage was somewhat unfortunate, the three caravels having to contend against terrible tempests.

Nevertheless they reached the Arguin Isles, and then the coast of this region, where they made twenty-five or more captives.

As they were sailing along the coast, having passed the islands, they beheld a man who was making signs to them from the shore. They thought at first that this was some native; but soon they had the joy of recognizing their fellow-countryman João Fernandes, whom they took on board and carried back to the kingdom. He had remained seven months in these parts, and in another chapter the author recounts the intelligence which he had obtained.

This João Fernandes, who was personally known to the author, had already been a captive among the Moors of the Mediterranean coast, and had there learned Arabic and Berber; and knowing these tongues, and having also some knowledge of the interior of Africa, he had charged himself with the mission of learning more by dwelling for a time among the natives of Rio do Ouro.

During this same voyage Antão Gonçalves treated with a Moorish knight, Ahude Meyman, for the purchase of some negroes of Guinea whom he was holding in captivity. This Moor came aboard the caravel, as did many others, and above all some women who were anxious to see the ship. They chose divers objects which pleased them and were of little value to the Portuguese, and in exchange they gave

the Portuguese nine negroes. This was the first
purchase of captives made by the Portuguese, and
this cape was given the name of Cabo do Resgate
(purchase).[1]

These same caravels proceeded to Cape Blanco,
where they made yet another capture of sixty Moors—
men, women, and children.

And these caravels were the first which, on returning
from the western coast of Africa, entered the estuary
of the Tagus and disembarked their captives in
Lisbon. The author describes the great excitement in
the city, and the crowd which gathered to see the
landing of the captives . . .

. . .

The arrival in Lisbon of the caravels of Antão
Gonçalves with the captives made a great impression.
To hear a matter recounted is one thing; to see,
another. The labour of the Infante at Lagos, his
perseverance for so many years, though at first
criticized and even censured, and then—as his success
became apparent—admired, did not truly find its full
justification in the general opinion until Lisbon was
able to see with its own eyes this procession of Moorish
and negro captives, this *black gold* which represented
so great a treasure. The city of Lagos and the dockyards of the Infante's school of navigation were in
Algarve, too far from Lisbon; communications were
difficult, and it was rarely that any went thither.
Azurara says:

As the city of Lisbon is the noblest in the realm
of Portugal, so its inhabitants—taking the greater part
for the whole—are most noble and most wealthy . . .

[1] This cape is marked with this name in the manuscript maps already
mentioned. In a large Portuguese map on parchment in the Bibliothèque
Nationale it is marked *P (Porto) do Resgate*. This name was adopted in
all the Portuguese hydrogeographic charts, giving the data for the
nomenclature of the maps of all European nations.

When these people saw the wealth which the ships had brought back, acquired in so short a time, and, seemingly, with such ease, some asked themselves in what manner they too could acquire a share of these profits . . .

The first who undertook this voyage from Lisbon was a certain Gonçalvo Pacheco, issued from a noble family, reared by the Infante, who had become chief treasurer of the affairs of Ceuta; he was a man of might, the possessor of armed ships, which he sent to sea to fight the enemies of the faith.

He readily secured the Infante's permission, and set sail with a little fleet of three caravels, having chosen for his captains Diniz Eannes da Grã, Alvaro Gil, and Mafaldo.

They sailed as far as Cape Blanco, and then to Arguin, where they took fifty captives with some difficulty and danger.

Continuing on their way southward, they left Tider[1] thirty-five leagues behind them, and discovered a cape to which they gave the name of Sant'Anna,[2] beyond which they found an arm of the sea about four leagues in length. Alvarro Vasques, accompanied by some of his men, followed on foot the shore of this gulf (which they took at first for a river) for a distance of a league and a half; and finding a village in their path, they attacked it and brought back thirty-five prisoners.[3]

[1] On the map of West Africa in the atlas already cited Tider is shown to the south of Arguin.

[2] *Cabo*, or rather *Golfo de Sant'Anna*. This name (like others which we have indicated) was adopted for the nomenclature of the hydro-geographical charts of the fifteenth, and even of the seventeenth, century.

[3] From Cape Blanco to Senegal the coast of which Azurara speaks is inhabited by various tribes of half-caste Moors, who speak Arabic and are Mohammedans: *Trazas* or *Teraryahs*, *Brakanas*, and others. They are a rather ferocious people.

With the three caravels they continued on their way southward, sailing eighty leagues beyond this Cape (or Gulf of) Sant'Anna; and so they came to the coast of Guinea.[1] On the shore they saw armed natives, but they could not disembark, since a tempest arose, against which they had to struggle for three days. However, they saw both men and cattle on the green and fertile coast.

The tempest obliging them to put about, they returned towards Tider. Once more they disembarked (thirty-five men in the ship's boats) and had to fight against fifty Moors, armed with lances, whom they overcame, and among whom they made prisoners.

Although they already possessed a goodly number of captives, and had sailed beyond the known territories, they wished once more to try their luck, and continuing along the coast they explored some of the bays between Cape Blanco and Cabo de Tira.[2]

They explored the sandbanks and islands of sand between the Arguin Isles and the point of Senegal. And having found on one of these islands some turtles bound with cords, and perceiving by this sign that the natives would come back for them, they made ready to fight them. But this time fate was unfavourable to them. The natives came down upon them suddenly in very great numbers, and seven Portuguese found their death there, and the others contrived to escape in their boats and return to the caravels. And Azurara adds: . . .

And some say that they had heard it said by some of the Moors of this place who were afterwards captured by us that their companions had eaten these dead men; and although others said the contrary to free their people from the reproach of a thing so

[1] That is, a little beyond Cape Verde.
[2] It would seem that Cabo de Tira (which is not marked on any map) must be a promontory at the mouth of the Senegal River,

monstrous, it is certain nevertheless that it is their custom to eat one another's livers and drink one another's blood; and that they do this by way of vengeance when their parents or children or brothers are slain. And it seems to me that there is no doubt in this respect, because in the book of Marco Polo it is said that these things were customary among many of the people of these regions.[1]

After this the three caravels of Gonçalo Pacheco went to the Isle of Arguin in order to make ready for their return to Portugal.

. . .

. . . Lançarote, the knight, and the King's treasurer in Lagos, went to the Infante, accompanied by the judges, the alcade, and the councillors of the city; and they said to him:

"Your Highness knows how the inhabitants of our city, from the taking of Ceuta to the present time, have always fought, and are fighting now, risking their persons and their ships in the war against the Moors, in the service of God and the King our lord. And even in the days of other kings, when the coast of this realm was ravaged by the Moors, our ships were ever the first to arm against them, as is recounted in writing and preserved in the memory of very aged men. In our days, Lord, since you ordained the search

---

[1] Azurara, having written this chronicle in 1453, must have read a manuscript copy of the *Travels of Marco Polo*; perhaps the copy which the Infante Dom Pedro brought back from Venice. The oldest edition of the travels is that of 1484. This book, which had great influence as regards the discoveries of the Portuguese, was read by the Portuguese scholars from the beginning of the fifteenth century, and one of its earliest translations is the Portuguese version published by Valentine Fernandes, together with the *Voyage of Nicolas the Venetian*, etc., dedicated to the King Dom Manuel (Lisbon, 1503, one vol., infolio Gothic).

for these lands of Guinea, you know well that it was here that you caused to be armed the greatest number of ships, and it was here that you found the aid which it was in our power to give you. Thus, Lord, since after the obedience we owe to the King your nephew and our lord, it is you that we are bound most chiefly to love, we have considered what should be the manner of serving you specially, and in such wise that by the merit of our actions we shall be honoured in the memory of men in the centuries to come; and even if we receive no other reward, this would suffice to us; but we are confident that in this we shall find great profit, and above all in the benefits which we shall receive, on our return, from your Highness.

"And in truth, Lord," they said, "matters are so that even after your death, and so long as this land shall be peopled, its inhabitants will pray to God for you. And even if some, by malice, would deny these things, the presence of your benefactions would contradict them, for every day they would have before their eyes the progeny of the servitors from whom they would have inherited, and in their houses abundance of bread, brought from the islands which you have peopled; and they would have the ancient writings which would tell of all the great privileges and liberties which you have granted them. Thus, Lord, we have considered all these things, and we see that you labour each time more strongly in the war against these Moors; we have learned how, at the time of Lançarote's expedition, they found many Moors in the Isle of Tider, where afterwards Gonçalo de Sintra was slain. We think, moreover, that the Moors of this island may prove an obstacle to your ships, and we desire, if you will deign to allow us, to arm our ships against them, and by death or imprisonment break their strength and their power, so that your vessels can navigate these parts without any danger. And if God wills that this undertaking shall end in our victory, we shall be able to make captures of great value, of which, from your fifth part, you will have great profit, of which we shall have our share. And we hope, Lord, soon to have your answer, in order that we may undertake our voyage while the summer allows."

. . .

The Infante at once gave his permission, and fourteen caravels were armed at Lagos, the command of which the Infante gave to Lançarote, which was a great honour considering the quality of the other captains. One of them, the father-in-law of Lançarote, alcade of the city, was called Sueiro da Costa; he was noble, and had been reared from childhood in the household of the King Dom Duarte; he had travelled and fought in Spain, France, and Italy; with King Ferdinand of Aragon against the people of Valencia, at the siege of Balaguer (1413); with Ladislas of Naples against Rome; with Louis II Count of Provence at the Battle of Agincourt; with the Comte de Foix at the taking of Soissons; and at the siege of Arras; and everywhere he had won distinction, and also at the taking of Ceuta. And among the captains there was also Alvaro de Freitas, commander of Aljezur, of the order of Santiago; noble also, and having bravely fought against the Moors of Granada; and Gil Eannes, who was the first to round Cape Bojador; and many more as good.

But over and above these fourteen caravels others left Lisbon with the same purpose, and also the Isle of Madeira. They were in all six and twenty; and they set sail all in this year of 1447. Those of Lagos weighed anchor all together on August 10th. But on the way they departed from one another, for their speed was not equal. And the ship of Laurenço Dias gained greatly upon the others, and was the first to arrive off the Arguin Isles.

The three caravels of Gonçalo Pacheco were still there. The voyage of these caravels had not been fruitless; they brought back many captives, and had gone beyond the regions known until that time. However, some of their men had found their death in the Isle of Tider while fighting against the Moors, and their return, by reason of this sorrow, was less joyous than it should have been.

Their grief, however, was somewhat lessened when they saw the sails of Laurenço Dias' caravel:

. . . because they knew that this ship could not be other than Christian, and could have come only from this Kingdom of Portugal, for no other ships sailed in these latitudes . . .

When they had related their adventures and hearkened to the news from their country, Laurenço Dias persuaded them to await the other caravels, so that they might all together avenge the death of their comrades.

They accordingly set sail for the Isle of Herons, where they awaited for three days the arrival of the other caravels, while abundantly victualling their ships, for there were very many herons here, and other great birds, and above all:

. . . certain birds, of which there are none in this kingdom, which are called croés, all white and larger than swans. Their bills are a *covado* and more in length, and of the breadth of three fingers; they are like chased scabbards, with great abundance of

ornament, as though they had been worked artificially
with the aid of fire in order to give them more beauty.
Their neck is so great that it can contain the leg of
a man, even of tall stature . . .[1]

Other caravels from Lagos joined them before long;
nine in all; which made thirteen, with that of
Laurenço Dias and the three of Gonçalo Pacheco.

They resolved to attack the Isle of Tider. They
found there Moors in great numbers, and armed;
they fought against them, killing eight and capturing
four; and the others fled. One Portuguese was
wounded and died some time thereafter.

The caravels of Gonçalo Pacheco, because they
were beginning to lack victuals, and also because they
were heavily laden with the captives already taken,
parted from the others and returned to Portugal,
where they arrived without further impediment.

The rest returned to the Isle of Tider, for they
were not fully content with their first expedition.[2]

[1] This bird is a hornbill, *Bucerus Nasutus*, Linn; Lathom calls it
Bucerus Africanus. The negroes of Senegal call it *Tock*, and the Portuguese
croé. Thus the bird was not first observed by P. Labat, as Buffon says.
Azurara gives a description of it—of course, exaggerated—based on the
information supplied by the Portuguese, who saw this bird in 1447,
three centuries before Labat observed it.

[2] At the beginning of Chapter LVI of this chronicle, in which this
second expedition to the Isle of Tider is described, the author cites a
passage of the *Regimine principium*, written in 1285 by Fr. Gil de Rome
for the edification of Philippe le Bel, King of France. This book had
a great renown towards the latter part of the fourteenth century and
during the fifteenth. Before the attack on Ceuta (1415) King Dom João I
recalled to the Portuguese knights the maxims of this book, which he
always had by him; and his son, the Infante Dom Pedro, made a
Portuguese version of it, which is one of the oldest, after the French
translation attributed to Henri de Gand.

Azurara's quotation reveals the state of erudition and literary culture
in Portugal at the beginning of the fifteenth century, and also the
literary relations which existed between Portugal and France, and other
countries, during the late Middle Ages.

They therefore set out for the Isle of Tider in their boats during the darkness, and coming to the harbour in the morning they perceived a multitude of armed Moors. The sea was so low at this point that the boats could not come at the shore. They leapt into the water and went forward at a walk; but soon they found themselves before a sort of deep channel which they could not cross save by swimming, and taking counsel for a moment they hesitated before this obstacle. The Moors regarded them; then, seeing them checked, they began to dance and sing as though they wished to mock their enemies . . .

. . . They [the Portuguese] thus found themselves in conflict with themselves, for their will commanded them to go forward, and fear held them back by showing to them this deadly peril. Now there was among them a gentleman of the Infante's household— whom I came to know thereafter, when he was already a noble knight—who had embarked in the quality of clerk in one of the caravels, for the Infante did not make any of his servants a squire without he had first distinguished himself by some feat of arms. Now this gentleman, who was called Diogo Gonçalves, seized with a great courage, demanded of a man of Lagos who was beside him . . . if he would keep him company, for he was about to strike out and swim. "By my faith," said the other, "you can demand of me nothing more pleasing." And these words were hardly spoken when he cast himself into the water, swimming, and the gentleman beside him . . .

Seeing which, the others also cast themselves forward and swam, first two or three, then many more, and lo and behold, they were all shortly battling against the Moors, who sought to prevent them from attaining the shore. The battle was perilous but not long protracted. The Portuguese had soon contrived to kill eight of the Moors, and thereat sought their safety in flight. But the Portuguese succeeded in making fifty-seven prisoners, and returned with these captives to the caravels.

They then set sail for Cape de Tira, and there took five Moors prisoner. After which, the captains being gathered in council, Gomes Pires, who commanded a caravel of the King's, proposed to them that they should continue their voyage southward:

". . . Because you, honoured lords and friends, know very well the great desire of the Infante to have intelligence concerning the land of the Negroes, especially concerning the River Nile . . .[1]"

Some of the captains, whose caravels were smaller, fearing the length and the perils of the voyage for their vessels, returned to Portugal, while six only pursued the voyage: those of Lançarote, Alvaro, Freitas, and others. They continued on their course along the coast, and . . .

. . . passed beyond the *Land of the Sahara*, of the Moors who are called Azanegues, which may readily enough be distinguished from the other, for there is much sand there, and no verdure to be seen; water is lacking there, which leads to much unfruitfulness. And to this land in general go all the swallows and all the birds which appear for a time in our kingdom,

---

[1] This passage, like many others in this chronicle, reveals the intentions and the system of the Infante Dom Henrique in respect of these expeditions. He wished not only to discover these territories, but above all to obtain through the natives information concerning the interior of Africa; in order to compare it with the scientific notions of antiquity and the Middle Ages, so that he could continue his discoveries until the Orient was reached.

such as storks, quails, turtle-doves, wrynecks, nightin-
gales, hedge-sparrows, and divers other birds. Many
leave these regions by reason of their heat; and others
leave them during the winter, such as falcons, herons,
rock-doves, thrushes, and other birds which make
their nests in these regions, and then come into our
kingdom, and this by reason of the food which they
find here according to their nature. And the men of
these caravels perceived many of these birds on the
sea, and others on the land engaged in building their
nests and feeding their young.

And since I am speaking on this subject, I wish to
say somewhat of the diversity of other birds and fishes
which there are in this region. Firstly, there are birds
which are called *framengos*, of the bigness of herons;
their neck is as long, but not thickly feathered, and
the head is in proportion to the greatness of the body;
but the bill is large, although short, and so heavy
that the neck can ill support it, so that it mostly
leans it against its legs and its feathers.[1] And other
birds, greater than swans, of which we have already
spoken, and which are called *croés*. There are also
fish which have beaks three or four *palmos*[2] in length,
some smaller, some larger; and these beaks have
teeth on either side, so close to one another that one
cannot lay a finger between them; and they are of
thin bone, and somewhat greater and something
farther apart than the teeth of a saw. These fish are
as great and sometimes greater than the sharks, and
their maw is not larger than that of other fish.[3] And

---

[1] *Phoenixoterus*, the flamingo.
[2] A *palmo* was about eight inches.
[3] *Pristis*.

there is also another fish,[1] no bigger than the mullet, which has upon the head a sort of crown by which it breathes, doing the office of gills, and if it is set in a basin with its crown against the bottom, it adheres thereto so strongly that on seeking to lift it you will lift the basin along with it, as happens with the mouth of lampreys if they are right lively.

And there are many other animals, birds, and fish in these regions of which we shall not give any description, since this would divert us from our subject.

[1] *Remora.* The "crown," or sucker is actually formed by the amalgamation of two fins; the fish does not breathe through it. (B. M.)

CHAPTER VI

*How Lançarote and his companions discovered the Nile
of the Negroes (Senegal). Other voyages, discoveries,
and adventures. How João Gonçalves Zarco sent out his
nephew Alvaro Fernandes, who discovered the Cap dos
Matos*

. . .

THESE six caravels of Lançarote's therefore pursued their course toward the south. Having passed
beyond the land of Sahara, as we have said, the
Portuguese saw the two palms which Diniz Dias had
already reported,[1] and they understood that here
began the Land of the Negroes, which caused them
great joy. They wished immediately to disembark,
but the sea was so rough that they could not. Some
of those who were there said thereafter that the
perfume which came from the land proved the rich-
ness of its fruits, for on coming to it by sea this perfume
gave them the impression that they had been brought
into a delightful orchard.

And if our men were envious to disembark, those
on land showed themselves no less desirous of receiving
them; but of their hospitality I shall not speak, for,
to judge by their first demonstrations, their intentions

[1] These palms are marked in the old MS. charts. Barros, another
chronicler, says: "Lançarote . . . came in sight of the two palms
which Dinis Fernandes [Dias], when he was there, had noted as a thing
remarkable . . . where the natives say that the Moorish Azenegues are
parted from the idolatrous negroes. . . . It is a fact that this river
marks the division between the Moors or Berbers who inhabit the
northern bank and the Yaloffos negroes who inhabit the southern bank."
(*Vide* DURAND, v. ii, p. 60, and RENNELL, *Appendix*, p. 80.)

were in no wise peaceful. The inhabitants of this green land[1] are all black; and for this reason the land is called the Land of the Negroes or Land of Guinea, and the men and women who inhabit it are called *Guineus*, which is to say blacks, negroes.

When the men in the caravels saw the first palms, and the tall trees of which we have already spoken, they knew that they were near the River Nile, where it casts itself into the sea of the Ponent, and which is called the River of *Canaga*. For the Infante had told them that when they had passed the trees, having sailed a little more than twenty leagues farther, they should look for the river; such was the intelligence which he had contrived to secure from some of the captive Azenegues.

And as they regarded the shore, hoping to perceive the river, they saw before them, at some two leagues distance from the land, a track in the sea of water of a different colour, and it was the colour of clay. They believed that there were shoals in this place, and they took soundings for the safety of their ships, but they found no difference of depth, which astonished them greatly. It then so chanced that one of those who was casting the lead carried his wet hand to his mouth, and he noted that the water was fresh.

"Here is a new marvel," he declared to the others; "this water is fresh!"

Then they drew the water in a bucket and tasted it, and all drank of it, and they found that it was good.

"Surely," they said, "we are near the River Nile,

[1] In the MS. map of João Freire (1546) the wood of which Azurara speaks is marked at the mouth of the Senegal River.

for this water seems to be the water of that river; its current, which is very strong, cuts through the sea in just such a manner."[1]

They made signals to the other caravels, and all sought the mouth of the river, which they found at no great distance . . .

They cast anchor and sent a boat ashore with Estavam Affonso, a squire of the Infante's, and seven men. They found a hut, in which they captured a young man who was wholly naked, and who carried a short lance, and his sister, who may have been eight years of age.

. . .

. . . This young negro was afterwards educated according to the orders of the Infante, and he was taught all such things as a Christian should know— and many a Christian does not know them as well as this young negro knew them. He was taught the *Pater Noster* and the *Ave Maria* and the articles of the faith and the precepts of the law and the works of mercy, and many other things beside, for the purpose of the Infante was to give him such instruction as would enable him to become a priest, so that he might preach the faith of Jesus Christ in his own country . . .

The Portuguese, after making this capture, went into the hut, and there found a black buckler, round, and somewhat larger than those which are used in

---

[1] This error of the Portuguese navigators, who confused the Senegal with the Nile, is yet another proof of the influence of the systematic geography of the ancients. According to Pliny, the Niger was a branch of the Nile. The River Senegal crosses a region almost nine hundred miles in width from its source in the Fouta highlands to the Atlantic. *Vide* DURAND, *Voyage au Sénégal*, p. 343, and DEMANET, *Nouvelle Histoire de l'Afrique*, vol. i, p. 62, *et seq.*

this realm, which had in the centre a boss carved out
of the leather itself; and this buckler was made out
of an elephant's ear, as was recognized afterwards by
some *Guineus* who saw it; and they declared that all
their bucklers were made of the hide of this beast;
and this leather is so thick that they cut away the
half of its thickness, which they do by thinning it
with instruments which they have made for the
purpose. The same negroes say further that the
elephants are so great that their flesh will suffice to
satisfy five hundred men, and that they find it very
good, and that the bones are not utilized in any
manner, and are even thrown away. But I have
learned that in the Levant, on the Mediterranean
coast, the bones of one of these beasts are currently
worth a thousand *dobras*.[1]

When they had taken the young negro and his
sister they put them into the boat, and Estavam
Affonso with his men went forth to search for the
parents. They heard the blows of an axe, and pro-

[1] It will be seen that at this time Azurara was aware only of the
trade in ivory which was carried on through the Levantine seaports of
the Mediterranean. As a matter of fact, up to this period the trade
was carried on by the Arabs, who came through Egypt from the coast
of Zanzibar, where the best ivory was obtained. The Arab caravans
brought ivory also from the Niger country. (*Vide* MOSSONDI, *Notices et
extraits des Manuscrits de la Bibliothèque du Roi*, vol. i, p. 15; IBN OUARDI,
vol. i, p. 40, and vol. ii, pp. 35–37; BAKOUI, ibid., pp. 394 and 401.)

These exaggerated descriptions of birds and animals until then
unknown show the influence of the teratological traditions of antiquity
and the Middle Ages, due to the study of the figures painted on the
planispheres and maps of the period; they resulted also from the study
of Pliny, and above all of the *Treatise on Marvels* attributed to Aristotle,
whose authority was so great among the Portuguese of the fifteenth
century that the procurators of the people, in the Cortes of 1481, cited
his *Politics*.

ceeding in that direction Estavam Affonso bade his
men follow him at a distance, lest they alarm the
native, and went forward alone, creeping and hiding
himself in order to take the man by surprise . . .

. . . And thanks to the prudence with which he
went forward, and because the negro was attentive to
his work, the latter was aware of the other's approach
only when he leapt upon him. I say that he leapt upon
him, for Estavam Affonso was of small stature and
slight, and the negro was neither, but the contrary.
And the Portuguese seized him so strongly by the
hair that when the negro raised himself Estavam
Affonso remained suspended in the air. The Guineu
was valiant and sturdy, and it seemed to him a
vexatious thing to be thus held by a creature so small;
in amazement he asked himself what it could be. But
on putting forth the greatest efforts he could not free
himself; the Portuguese had so fastened upon his hair
that the struggle between the two was like the boldness
of an infuriated greyhound hanging upon the ear of
a mighty bull.

To speak the truth, it already seemed to Estavam
Affonso that the help of the others was long in coming;
I believe that his heart repented of his first counsel,
and if at such a moment it had been possible to strike
a bargain, he would have held it profitable to lose
what he had gained in exchange for the security
which this loss would have procured for him.

The two being thus at grips, the others at length
came up, and they took the negro by the arms and
the neck to bind him. Estavam Affonso, believing that
he was already well held by the others, let go of his
hair, and the Guineu, feeling his head free, shook the

others off his arms, throwing each in a different direction, and fled. The pursuit of the Portuguese was fruitless, for in nimbleness the negro was greatly their superior; and he plunged into a dense wood, where his enemies, thinking to hold him, were still searching for him when he was already in his hut seeking his children and his weapons.

All that had hitherto befallen him was a little thing compared with the grief of perceiving that his children had disappeared; and harbouring yet a little hope, he looked from side to side, believing that they had hidden themselves and that he might discover them.

At this moment appeared Vicente Dias, captain of the caravel whose boat had put ashore. It seems that he was walking upon the beach, as it was his habit to do when he was in the city of Lagos, without other weapon than a boathook.

But the Guineu, so soon as he beheld him, being inflamed with rage, as you may well conceive he must have been, threw himself upon the captain with the greatest courage. Vicente Dias saw him thus coming, full of fury, and he understood that he had no weapons that would defend him; but flight would have advantaged him nothing, and, on the contrary, would even have been unfavourable to him; so that he awaited this other without showing any fear. And the Guineu, coming upon him swiftly at a run, struck at his face with his lance and laid open his whole jaw; and immediately the negro received another wound, albeit less than that which he had dealt. As their weapons were but trifling things for such a combat, they flung themselves at each other and had recourse to their hands. Grappling with each other they struggled as best they could. At this moment another negro came up—a youth—who hastened to the aid of the first; and although the first negro was so strong and so valiant, he would surely have been taken had not the other arrived, which obliged Vicente Dias to leave his first enemy in order to confront the second.

The other Portuguese then came up, but the Guineu finding himself rid of his enemy, the two negroes, like men well used to running, took to flight, having then no fear of the enemies who pursued them.

And at length our men returned to the caravels with the petty capture which they had kept in their boat . . .

The captains wished again to go ashore and seek a new opportunity of taking captives, and of increasing their knowledge of that region, but the wind being contrary they had perforce to return to Cape Verde. In these latitudes they encountered some of the other caravels, and sailing together they discovered an island, on which they landed; it was not inhabited, but there were on it great numbers of wild goats, "which were like those of the kingdom, the difference being only in the ears, which were longer." Of these they took some for their victualling, and also water.

And they discovered yet another island, and on it they saw the arms of the Infante, and his device, carven upon the bark of a tree; and they understood that one of their caravels, or several, had already passed that way.

As there was a great multitude of negroes on the shore they could not disembark; and these negroes attacked them with their arrows and their javelins, of which they carried back to the Infante a considerable quantity.

. . . and the arrows have no feathers, nor yet a notch to hold the bowstring, and they are all smooth and polished and short, made of rush or reed; the iron points are long, and fitted into recesses which are cut in the shafts, and they resemble the spindles which our women employ in spinning; and they have little barbs. All these arrows are poisoned with herbs. And the javelins have each seven or eight sets of barbs, and their herb is right venomous.

In this island, where the arms of the Infante were carven upon the trunk of a tree, they found strange trees, very great in the trunk, among which there was one whose trunk measured 108 *palmos*.[1] Of this tree the trunk is not very tall, no taller than a walnut-tree; from its bark they obtain fibres of which they make cords, and it burns like flax. Its fruits resemble calabashes, whose seeds are as big as walnuts. The natives eat the fruits when they are green, and they dry the seeds, of which they have great abundance, to eat them, I conceive, when they have no more fresh fruits.[2]

Some of these sailors declared that they had seen birds which seemed to be parrots.[3]

. . .

The caravels essayed once more to enter the River

---

[1] About 72 feet, the *palmo* being approximately eight inches.

[2] The baobab. The Portuguese navigators and Azurara described this tree three hundred and ten years before the French naturalist who gave it the botanical name by which it is known to-day. (*Adansonia digitata*: one of the silk-cotton trees. The fresh fruit is known as monkey-bread.)

[3] These islands are plainly marked between Cabo Verde and Cabo dos Matos on the curious map of Africa in the unpublished Atlas of Vaz Dourado (1571). (*Vide* ADMIRAL ROUSSIN, *Mém. sur la navigation aux côtes occidentales de l'Afrique*, p. 6.)

Nile, but they could not come at it; one of their number, that of Gomes Pires, having lost the others, went to make provision of water on the Isle of Arguin, and thereafter ascended the *Rio do Ouro* as far as the harbour to which this captain had gone the previous year, with Antão Gonçalves and Diogo Affonso. And the Moors came immediately, saying that no merchant was there at that moment.

They sold the Portuguese a negro, and brought them water and meat. They showed themselves very confident, and came aboard the caravel in great numbers, and the Portuguese let them depart without doing them any harm. It was agreed with these Moors that the Portuguese would return the following year, in the month of July, to this same place, and that they would find there many negroes to buy, and gold dust, and other merchandise.

Gomes Pires loaded his ship with many pelts of sea-wolves; he then returned to Portugal.[1]

.   .   .

The influence of the systematic geography of the ancients on the imaginations of the Portuguese of the fifteenth century was so great that when they came to the Senegal, and found fresh clear water at the mouth of this river, and other features which the ancients had described as particularities of the Nile, they did not doubt for a moment that they had found the Nile of the Negroes (the Niger).

What Azurara has to say on this subject affords proof of his great learning, and at the same time gives evidence of the historical and cosmographical know-

[1] From these passages and others we see that the commercial relations of the Portuguese with the West Coast of Africa beyond Cape Bojador had been established before the middle of the fifteenth century. This import trade consisted mainly of gold dust, slaves, and seal pelts.

ledge of the first Portuguese navigators. We shall call the reader's attention to one very important detail: if Azurara appears to be thoroughly familiar with what the ancients had written on this subject, the Portuguese navigators, while they shared this knowledge, show that they were also acquainted with the opinions of the Arab geographers. They gave the same name to the two rivers; nevertheless, they distinguished them: the Nile of Egypt, the Nile of the Negroes. The opinion that the Niger was a branch of the Nile was maintained even in the nineteenth century by Jackson in his book, *An Account of the Empire of Marocco and the District of Suze.*

In vol. xiv of the *Annales des Voyages* by Malte Brun, 1811, and in vol. xviii of the same work, we find a curious analysis of Jackson's arguments as to the identity of the two rivers.

After this voyage of Lançarote's, and the good results obtained, many ships set sail from Portugal, one after another, and several chapters of Azurara's chronicle are devoted to them, containing a minute account of their adventures and their successes or disasters. We shall select some of the more interesting passages of these narratives, which bear too much resemblance to deserve reproduction in full.

In chapter 67 Azurara relates how the officers of five caravels which sailed in company decided to explore the arm of the sea, or river, which they had seen near Cape Blanco. Having anchored at the mouth of this river, they ascended it in their boats for a distance of four leagues, reaching the end of it.[1] . . . Chapters 68 and 69 relate the adventures of the two caravels of Tavilla and Picanço, which had

---

[1] Concerning the position of this inlet, see the map by Anville published in LABAT, *Nouvelle relation de l'Afrique*, vol. i; and ROUSSIN, *Mém sur la navigation aux côtes occidentales de l'Afrique*, p. 44; and what is said in this latter book of the *Baie du Lévrier*, which is twenty miles in length from north to south and fifteen in width. This bay, which our navigators traversed, lies to the north of Cape Sant'Anna.

left the others before the latter continued on their voyage to Guinea.

On their return to Portugal they met the caravel of Alvaro Gonçalves d'Athayde, whose captain was João de Castilha, who was making toward Guinea. The two first-named captains persuaded him against making this voyage, since the season for such an expedition was over. They agreed to go in company to the Canaries, where they would endeavour to take some captives.

. . .

. . . And proceeding thus in company, they came to the Isle of Gomera, and wishing to disembark they saw a great number of Canarians, from whom they had guarantees of security before they landed. These guarantees were given without difficulty, as offered by men more desirous of welcoming than of repulsing the strangers. Two captains of this island came to meet them, saying that they were servants of the Infante; they had reason to say so, for they had already been at the Courts of the King of Castile and the King of Portugal, and nowhere had they been received and loaded with benefits as by the Infante; for being in his house they found there, during their whole sojourn, a right good welcome, and this prince had given them goodly raiment, and had sent them home in his own ships; and for this reason they were ready to do him service . . .

The captains of the caravels required them to aid them in an expedition which they desired to make to the Isle of Palma, in order there to capture a few men, for they knew neither this island nor its inhabitants, nor their manner of fighting. And the two Canarian captains, Bruco and Piste, replied that they would be only too happy thus to aid them and serve the Infante.

Accordingly Piste, one of these chiefs, embarked with the Portuguese, taking as many men as ours desired, and they set sail at dawn for the Isle of Palma, and they resolved to land immediately, so that the natives might not have time to escape.

. . .

. . . And marching thus, not too far from the shore, they saw the Canarians, who were fleeing . . .

. . . But the Christians, as well as the Portuguese Canarians, made after them; and when the first began to enter the valley the others were already hard upon them, in such wise that the shepherds ran upon the rocks, so sharp and steep that it was a marvel to see them; but a far greater marvel was the sure and nimble fashion in which these Canarians leapt upon these perilous rocks . . .

In this chase the Portuguese, who were not accustomed to this sort of exercise, could with difficulty follow their enemies. One of them even slipped, and falling was killed. And the same thing happened to several of the natives in their haste to escape by a path so perilous.

. . .

. . . The travail of our men was very painful this day; the combat was perilous; the Canarians cast stones at them, these being their chiefest weapons, which serve them well, by reason of the strength of their arms and the exactness of their aim; they can hardly be hurt by their enemies, for they contrive to avoid the projectiles by twisting their bodies, and it is very rarely that one can touch them. They have also other weapons consistent with their brutish life;

long lances, having pointed horns in place of iron
points . . .

Despite all these difficulties the Portuguese contrived to capture this day seventeen Canarians, men
and women; among them was a woman of immoderate
size, who, it seemed, was the queen of a portion of
the island.

This chief, Piste, with others of this island of
Gomera, came afterwards to Portugal, and they were
very well received by the Infante, who gave them
many presents.

. . .

. . . And this I can certify, for I was in the province
of Algarve with the prince at the time when these
Canarians were there, and I saw well how he treated
them.

. . .

The captain of one of these caravels, João de
Castilha, was by no means content with this capture
of Canarians, and persuaded the others to take yet
more by treachery. They therefore presented themselves as friends at another harbour of this same
island of Gomera, and the natives having come on
board in all confidence, they took twenty-one of them
and carried them off. But when they arrived in
Portugal the Infante, having knowledge of what had
passed, waxed extremely wroth against these captains,
and sending for the Canarians to come to his house
gave them fine raiment and sent them back to their
island . . .

Diniz Dias, as we have already said, armed a
caravel belonging to D. Alvaro de Castro, and his
companion was Pallenço, who embarked on a flatboat.
Pallenço had no intention of using this little boat for
any other purpose than to enter the River Nile; for

it was old, and he had resolved to abandon it wherever he saw that its last hour of service had come.

Pursuing thus the course of their voyage, they came to the Isle of Arguin, where they took in supplies of water, and there they resolved to continue their voyage to the Land of the Negroes, according to their intention on leaving the kingdom. And having some time before passed the Cape of Sant'Anna,[1] after a day of great heat Pallenço was of the mind that it would be no ill thing to land a few men who should essay to take some of the Moors.

"Why," said Diniz Dias, "do we concern ourselves with such a matter? Let us continue on our course, for, if God leads us to this land of Guinea, we shall there find Moors in abundance for our cargo."

That which Diniz Dias said was true, for there were many Moors, but they were not so easy to take as he believed, for they were men right strong and skilled in defence, as you shall see in the following chapters, where we shall speak of their combats (against our men).

"Friend," replied Pallenço, "even if this be so, even if we there find many Moors, what shall we lose if God wishes to give us some few here? I am of a mind that we should essay to take some, and it may be that God will permit us to take so many that we shall have no need to go farther."

"Since the matter stands there," said Diniz Dias, "do you give your orders as you may require."

Pallenço straightway made ready to put ashore with his flatboat; but although the weather was very

---

[1] *Ponta de Santa-Anna.* To the south of the River S. João in the chart of João Freire (1546).

hot, the waves were so great on the coast that the flatboat could not draw near the shore. Pallenço, however, desirous of pursuing to a good end what he had undertaken, said to the men who were with him:

"Friends, you see that the fierceness of this sea towards the shore does not permit our boat to reach the land. My desire would be to disembark none the less, but as I cannot swim it would be folly to do this. If among you there are some who would wish to go ashore by swimming, I should be under a great obligation to you, and you would by no means lack the praises which the brave merit by their exploits."

Some replied to him:

"Our desire to please you is very great; but see, we have before us two perils: the first is the uncertainty of reaching the shore, for these waves may torment us in such a manner that being no longer master of our limbs we shall be killed, for such things have already come to pass; the second peril is that if we come on shore and there find men with whom we shall have to fight without your aid, if the sea is such that you cannot disembark, what shall we do?"

However, as you know that where there are many men together opinions differ; while Pallenço was hearkening to these words, other men would not even give ear to the latter part of this conversation, and having gone off to the other end of the flatboat, of a sudden they came all naked before Pallenço and made ready to cast themselves into the water.

"Here are we," they said; "do you give us your orders, for there is but one death for each man, and if God has resolved that we shall die in His service, this occasion is the best for finding the end of our life."

And immediately, having received the orders of their captain, they loaded themselves with their clothes and their weapons as best they could, and launched themselves forward swimming. Although the sea was very bad, it pleased God that they should be saved; and all twelve of those who had started came to the shore.

They marched along the coast, and soon he who went before called to the others to halt, for he saw the imprints of men's feet, and it seemed to him that these imprints were quite fresh . . .

.   .   .

From this adventure they returned all safe and sound, and brought with them six captives whom they were able to embark. They continued their southward voyage, but before long it was found that the flatboat was unfit for service, and removing all their possessions to the caravel they abandoned the boat.

Soon after this the caravel of Diniz Dias encountered that of Rodrigo Eannes Travassos, and they sailed on in company. They came to Cape Verde, and laid up a store of water at the islands.[1]

On one of these islands Diniz Dias landed by night with two men to make a reconnaissance; and on returning to the caravels he said:

"It would not be wise if we were to seek a battle against these people here, for I have found a very large village divided into two parts, and you know well that the people of this country are difficult to take; the men are strong and quick and good warriors, and their arrows are poisoned with a very dangerous

---

[1] These are probably the islands marked in some maps—and especially French maps—as *Isles de la Madeleine.*

herb. Therefore it seems to me that we should let them be, for all our efforts would result only in our death . . ."

. . . Diniz Dias said that he had seen something in this island that seemed to him a new thing; among the cows he had seen two animals which compared with the other cattle were very strange; although they were mingled with the herd, Diniz Dias believed that they must be *bufaros*[1] . . .

. . .

They therefore returned to the place where they had abandoned the flatboat, thinking that the negroes would have gone thither to retrieve the wreck.

They sent ashore twenty men. The negroes hid themselves and set an ambush, whence ensued a perilous and most unequal battle, in which, however, the Portuguese contrived to gain the victory.

After this they once more tried their luck by landing at the Ponto de Tira; but they brought off only one Moor as testimony of their efforts . . .

. . .

I have still to tell the story of what befell the caravel of João Gonçalves Zarco, who, to my thinking, was he who in this adventure undertook it in the most disinterested spirit; for all the others, despite their goodwill to serve the Infante, had also, as you have seen, the hope of profit before their eyes. But this João Gonçalves Zarco was noble in all that he undertook, and it was well known that he ordered this voyage only for the service of his lord the Infante. Arming a very goodly caravel, to which he appointed

---

[1] The African buffalo.

as captain one of his nephews, whom the Infante had reared in his household, and who was called Alvaro Fernandes, he recommended him to entertain no thought of profit other than that of seeing and learning some new thing; and he required him neither to stop nor to make reconnaissance in the land of the Moors, but to go directly to the land of the negroes, and to sail beyond it as far as he was able, contenting himself with returning to Portugal empty-handed, but bringing the Infante some news which would give him pleasure.

The caravel was well equipped and provided, the ship's company chosen from among men who were brave and ready for all dangers; and Alvaro Fernandes, their captain, was a strong and valiant young man.

They accordingly followed their route, resolved to obey him who had sent them forth; and thus they sailed upon the great ocean until they came to the River Nile,[1] where they drew two barrels of water, of which they took one back to Lisbon. And I do not know whether Alexander, who was one of the monarchs of the world, ever drank water which had been brought from so great a distance!

They passed this river, and beyond Cape Verde they saw an island, on which they disembarked in the hope of finding inhabitants, but with the prudence that ought to be exercised in these regions.[2]

And on searching the island they found tame

---

[1] The Senegal, or "Nile of the Negroes."

[2] This island must be Gorée, which is situated in 14° 39′ 55″ N. lat. *Vide* DEMANET, *Nouvelles histoire de l'Afrique*, vol. i, pp. 87–97; *passim, Notices statistiques sur les colonies françaises* (3d. part, pp. 187–9), published by the Ministry of Marine in 1839.

goats, but no one to tend them, and no sign of habitation . . .

. . .

. . . And they continued their voyage to the place where stood the palm and the great tree of which we have spoken in other chapters.

. . .

They cast anchor near this cape, and there the negroes came to them as friends, and the Portuguese allowed them to come on board, received them well, and allowed them to depart; later these negroes returned in their boats in great numbers to attack them. The Portuguese defended themselves, and with much difficulty took two of the negroes.

They then went still farther, and came to a cape where there were many dead and leafless palms. And they gave this cape the name of *Cabo dos Matos*.[1]

And still farther on Alvaro Fernandes sent off in the ship's boat seven men, bidding them follow the coast; and they, rowing near the shore, saw four negroes who were sitting beside the sea. They leapt ashore and approached so softly that the natives did not detect their presence. When they were near enough they ran upon them to take them. These negroes were hunters armed with bows. When they saw the Portuguese, not having time to seize their bows, they fled as fast as they could. The Portuguese took their bows, arrows, and quivers, and a good provision of the flesh of wild swine which the negroes were cooking. But they could not secure the men, "for they were all naked, and their hair is very short, so that there was nothing which could give their enemies hold of them."

Of animals they saw one, a female, which was like

---

[1] This cape is so named in almost all the MS. charts of the sixteenth century. The name, as we see, was given to it by Alvaro Fernandes.

a roe, and was tame; it was probable that the negroes had it with them in order to attract "venison."[1]

They went no farther, and returned to the island of Madeira, and thence to the kingdom, where they were very well received and rewarded by the Infante.

And this was the caravel which that year went farther than all the rest along the African coast.

. . .

[1] Doubtless an antelope; for "venison," read herds of antelopes.

CHAPTER VII

Of the things which João Fernandes learned during his journeys with the caravans, and other details concerning these new African countries

TO aid in the understanding of these matters we shall now relate what befell João Fernandes,[1] who sojourned in these countries for seven months, in the service of the Infante, as you already know.

João Fernandes, having remained with the kinsfolk of that Moor whom Antão Gonçalves brought to our country, went off in their company, taking with him some raiment, some biscuits, and some wheat which was left of his provisions; all these things were immediately taken from him, against his will, and he was given only a woollen cape such as the Moors wear. These men were shepherds who were going to their own country.[2]

He related that this country was very sandy, without any grass, excepting in the valleys or low plains, where there was a little grass on which the flocks grazed scantily. But there are hills and mountains entirely of sand. This country of the Tagarz[3] extends

[1] See Chapter v.

[2] In this recital of João Fernandes, which is extremely interesting, above all because it antedates by almost a century the description of LEO AFRICANUS, it lacks what should have been the most important detail: the itinerary followed and the places visited during the seven months of his travels with the caravans. Nevertheless, the accuracy of his descriptions was confirmed by what LEO AFRICANUS and other travellers wrote later.

[3] This is the *Tagaza* of CADOMOSTO, and the *Tagazza* of JACKSON, on the way from Akka to Timbuctoo.

as far as the Land of the Negroes, and as far as the Mediterranean Sea, to the border of the Kingdom of Tunis, and to *Mondébarque.*

Hence this extent of country, such as I have described it, continues from the Mediterranean Sea to the Land of the Negroes, and to Alexandria; and everywhere it is peopled by men who are shepherds, in a greater or less degree, according as the land has more or less pasturage for bestial; there are no trees there, save such as are very small, as the cactuses, the nopals or Barbary fig-trees, the thorny paliurus, and occasionally palms.[1] There is no water but that of the wells;[2] there are no rivers and no streams, save in very few parts. The width of this country is perhaps three hundred leagues, and its length one thousand; and in it there is no place of importance, excepting Alexandria and Cairo.

The writing of these people[3] and their language are not like those of the other Moors; but they all belong to the sect of Mohamet, and they are called Alarves and Azenegues and Berbers.[4] And all dwell, as I have already said, in tents, with their flocks and herds, where they please, without any rule or law of property, or justice; each lives as he wills, and does as he pleases as far as is in his power.

They fight against the negroes, more by cunning

---

[1] *Vide* DENHAM and CLAPERTON.

[2] See the itineraries already cited and published in the work by M. WALCKENAER, *Recherches sur l'interieur de l'Afrique*, and the *Description of Africa* by LEO AFRICANUS.

[3] This detail is interesting, as it shows that in the fifteenth century, when Fernandes travelled with the caravans, some of these tribes—who were, we imagine, Berbers—had not yet adopted Arabic characters.

[4] According to BURCHARDT, p. 64 and p. 207, they are Berbers. Azurara includes the Libyans among these tribes.

than by strength, for they are very much weaker than they.[1]

Some Moors come into this country and buy the negroes whom these people have stolen; they carry them away forthwith and sell them at Mondébarque, which is at the frontier of the Kingdom of Tunis, to the Christian merchants who resort thither; they exchange them against bread and other things, as is done in these days on the *Rio do Ouro*, as I shall recount later.

And you must know that in all this land of Africa, which extends from Egypt to the Ponent, the Moors have no other kingdom than that of Fez, which contains the realms of Morocco and Tafilalet, and that of Tunis, which contains the realms of Tlemcen and Bugia. All the rest of the country belongs to these Alarves and Azenegues, who are shepherds, on foot or horseback, and who, as I have said, have no fixed habitation.

It is related that in the Land of the Negroes there is another kingdom, which is called Meelly; but this is not certain,[2] for they carry off the negroes of this kingdom and sell them like the others, which they would not do if they were Moors.

Returning to the adventures of João Fernandes: he travelled with these shepherds; in their company he traversed these sandy territories, and he was not always given enough milk to nourish him.

---

[1] It seems that Fernandes is speaking here of the Touaregs and their skirmishes with the Fulla negroes.

[2] It will be seen that Azurara did not believe in the existence of the great empire of Melle, very rich in gold-mines, although it had been visited in the previous century by the celebrated Arab traveller EBN-BATUTA.

One day it happened that he met two shepherds on horseback, who were going to the place where was that Ahude Meymon of whom we have spoken. And they inquired of João Fernandes if he wished to go along with them to find this Moor.

"I do indeed wish to do so," said João Fernandes, "for I have been told that he is a man of note, and I wish to make his acquaintance."

They then made him mount upon a camel, and set out for the place where they thought to find this Moor. They journeyed so long that the water began to fail them, and they were three days without drinking. It is said that in order to find this path they regarded the sky; and where they saw crows and certain other birds they understood that there were people, for in all this country there are no made roads except by the shore of the sea.

João Fernandes relates how the Moors with whom he was travelling were guided only by the winds, as at sea, and by these birds of which we have spoken.

And they journeyed on so long, enduring their thirst, that in the end they found this Ahude Meymon, with his sons and others who accompanied him; and there were close upon one hundred and fifty men. João Fernandes saluted the chief, and the Moor received him very well, and caused him to be given the food with which he nourished himself, which is to say milk, so that when the Portuguese was fetched off by the caravels he was well nourished and of a good colour.

João Fernandes says that the heat in this country is very great, and that there is much dust from the sands; that the people who go on foot are very numerous, and there are very few horsemen, for those that do not go on foot travel on camels; and some of these camels are white and can go fifty leagues in the day.[1] There are great numbers of these camels, not only white, but of other colours also; and many flocks, although the pastures are not abundant, as we have already said.

João Fernandes relates also that they have negro captives, and the more wealthy have much gold, which they bring from the country in which the negroes dwell; and that there are many ostriches, tapirs,[2] gazelles, and many partridges and hares. And the swallows which leave our country in the summer pass the winter among the sands, I conceive by reason of the heat they find there; and likewise other small birds; but the storks go to the Land of the Negroes, where they sojourn during the winter . . .

. . .

. . . Many of the people of Spain and other countries believed that the great birds which are called ostriches did not hatch their eggs, but that they laid them in the sand and abandoned them; which is false, as has been proved, for they lay twenty or thirty eggs and hatch them like other birds.

[1] This does not appear to be exaggerated. *Vide* RENNELL, "Memoir on the rate of travelling as performed by camels," in the *Phil. Trans.*, vol. 81, p. 144. Azurara is here speaking of certain camels of the desert and the Touareg country, whose gait is so rapid that they are able to travel in one day a distance which the ordinary camels would take ten days to cover. But these camels do not accompany the ordinary, regular caravans; they are used only for warlike excursions.

[2] It is difficult to guess what Azurara's tapir can be. I can only suggest that the report might be founded on a vague description of Burchell's rhinoceros, which still exists on the Upper Nile, and is more addicted to open country than other rhinoceri. (B. M.)

Those who are engaged in commerce in these countries traffic in many kinds of merchandise; negroes, whom they steal in great numbers; gold, which they seek in the Land of the Negroes; leather; wool; butter and cheese, of which they have a great deal; dates in great abundance, which come from other countries; amber, musk, copal, oil, and the pelts of seals, which abound in Rio do Ouro.

Also in this country the merchandise of Guinea may be had; and of this I shall speak later.

Up to this year of 1446 since the birth of Jesus Christ, fifty-one caravels have sailed from the kingdom and gone to these countries; but of the numbers of Moors whom they have brought back I shall not speak until the end of this book. These caravels rounded Cape Bojador and sailed 450 leagues beyond this cape; and it was found that this coast runs ever southward, and that it is all cut up by points of land and bays, such as the Infante has caused to be marked (in their true proportions) in the nautical charts. What was known of this coast of the Great Sea before these voyages was a stretch of 600 leagues, and to this 450 leagues have now been added. Whatever of this coast was marked upon the map of the world was not correct; it was indicated at hazard; but what is now marked upon the charts comprises only things seen, as I have already related . . .

. . . Now we must occupy ourselves with these countries to which our navigators have gone with so great labour and peril. And this to prove to you the error into which fell those who lived before us; which is to say, the fear of rounding Cape Bojador. And also that you may know what great praise the Infante

Dom Henrique merits for having dispersed these terrors of imaginary dangers, not only for us who have witnessed all his labours, but also for all who shall live after us in the future.

One of the great obstacles—so men believed—which hindered such voyages was the legend of terrible tides which existed in the sea, and against which no ship could struggle; you know now how false this was, since you have seen ships go and return without more danger to navigation than in any other seas whatsoever.

It was believed also that the lands were sandy and unpeopled; as for the sands, they were not altogether deceived; yet they were not such as men imagined. As for the notion that these lands were unpeopled, you see that just the contrary is the case, for now you have their inhabitants before your eyes every day. And as to the inhabited places, the greater number are villages; of cities or towns properly so-called there are very few; for from Cape Bojador to the Kingdom of Tunis there are not more than fifty towns or fortified places.

Men were likewise deceived as to the depth of the sea, for on the charts beaches were marked so flat that at a league from land there was no more than a fathom of water; and it was found, on the contrary, that the sea close inshore was so deep that vessels could navigate there . . . as you will find in the nautical charts which the Infante has caused to be prepared.[1]

---

[1] From all this portion of Azurara's text we see that the first hydrogaphic charts of the West Coast of Africa beyond Cape Bojador were made by the Portuguese by order of the Infante Dom Henrique.

In the Land of the Negroes there is no place
surrounded with walls other than that which they
call Oadem,[1] nor any village, except those which are
on the coast, although this territory is generally
populated; but these people pass their lives in their
tents and the carts [*sic*] which they use for transport
(as we do here when it happens that our princes are
on campaign with their armies), according to what
the captives have related, and also the recital of
João Fernandes.

The chief skill and care of these people is all in
the tending of their bestial, which is to say cows,
sheep, goats, and camels, and almost daily they move
their camp, and they do not remain longer than a
week in the same locality.

Among the chiefs there are some who possess mares
for breeding, but very few.

Their food is above all milk, and sometimes meat
and the seeds of wild grasses which they gather on
these hills; those who have been there say that these
grasses resemble the bird millet of our country; but
they are not plentiful.[2] They eat of wheat also when
they can get it, but it seems that they eat it as we
eat sweetmeats.[3] And for several months of the year

[1] This is probably the place which Cadomosto calls *Hodem* (Guaden):
"In the direction of Cape Blanco, in the interior, there is a village of
the name of Hodem, six days by camel from the coast. . . ." He adds
later: "It is not a village, but there the Arabs take shelter, and it serves
as a halting-place for the caravans which come from Tombouctou and
other places of the Negroes, towards our Barbary . . ."
This locality is marked, under Cadomosto's names, in the map of
caravan routes to be found in WALCKENAER's *Recherches geographiques sur
l'interieur de l'Afrique.*

[2] *Vide* the description given in the travels of CLAPERTON.

[3] *Itinéraire de Tripoli de Barbaire a la ville de Tombouctou,* by the SHEIKH
HAGG-KASSEM, published by M. Walckenaer, p. 425.

these people, as well as their horses and dogs, live only on milk. Those who dwell on the coast eat only fish and drink only water, and almost always they eat the fish raw and dried.

Their garments are a sort of jacket and breeches of leather; the more wealthy have often long capes of wool. The chiefs have good raiment like that of the other Moors, and good horses, handsome saddles, and fine stirrups; but those who possess these things are not numerous. The women wear capes of wool which are a sort of mantle with which they hide the face; and they conceive that they are thus hiding all that should not be revealed, for their bodies are naked. Certainly, says he who relates this story, this is one of the things that show the brutishness of man . . . The wives of the chiefs and headmen wear earrings and circlets of gold and other jewels.

CHAPTER VIII

*In which Azurara speaks of the Canary Isles, Madeira,
and the Azores*

IT seems to me that it is fitting to explain many
things in this book, for if I speak of them too
briefly those who should read the history would be
ill content at not learning all the particulars.

I have said that the Infante Dom Henrique sent
an expedition to the Canary Isles; and I have told
how after this the Portuguese ships went thither and
brought back captives.

I wish now to tell the number of these islands, and
how they are peopled, and what is the faith of these
folk, and all that has been learned concerning them.

According to what I have found in the ancient
writings of the time when there reigned in Castile
the King Don Henrique, son of the King Don Juan I,
who was defeated by the Portuguese in the Battle of
Aljubarrota,[1] a noble gentleman of France, who was
called Johann de Botancor,[2] and was a nobleman
and a Catholic desirous of serving God, knowing that
these isles belonged to the Infidels, left his country
with the intention of conquering them.

He proceeded to Castile, where he obtained ships,
and more men than he already had with him; and
on coming to these islands he had great difficulty in
conquering them. He succeeded in subjecting three,
and the other four were not conquered.

Johann de Botancor having spent all the money he

[1] 1385.   [2] Jean de Bethencourt.

had brought, and his supplies being exhausted, was obliged to return to his country, intending ere long to return and conquer the other islands. He left a nephew of his, called Maciote, as captain of the three islands already conquered.

But Johann de Botancor did not return; some say that he was prevented by grave maladies; others relate that he could not do so because the King of France required his services to aid him in the wars which he had undertaken.

And the aforesaid Maciote remained a long time in the Canary Isles; then he went to the island of Madeira, as I shall recount later.

These islands are now peopled as follows: in the island called *Lançarote* there are sixty men; in *Forte Ventura*, eighty; and in the other, called *Ferro*, twelve men. And these are the three which were conquered by this great seigneur of France. All these inhabitants are Christians, and perform their divine offices among themselves, having churches and priests.

But there is another island, called Gomera, which Maciote sought to conquer with the aid of some Castilians, but they could not succeed; among the inhabitants of this island are some who are Christians; and in all they are seven hundred.

In the Isle of *Palma* dwell five hundred men, and in the sixth, *Teneriffe* (called also the Isle of *Hell*, because there is a mountain there whose summit spews forth fire), there are six thousand warriors. The seventh island, called the Grand Canary, has fifty thousand warriors.

These three islands have never been conquered since the beginning of the world; but many of their

P

inhabitants have already been made prisoners, so that their manner of life is known; and because these things have seemed to me very different from the habits and customs of other peoples, I wish to say somewhat of them; for on reading me those who by divine mercy are liberated from so much brutishness will therefore render thanks to the Lord . . .

Of all these islands that I have named, the Grand Canary is the greatest; it measures thirty-six leagues about. The inhabitants are intelligent but not upright. They know that there is a God, and that those who do ill will suffer ill. Among them there are two whom they call kings, and a duke, but all the government of the island is in the hands of certain knights who are not fewer than one hundred and ninety nor more than two hundred. And when five or six of them die the others assemble and choose five or six new knights among their sons, for they may by no means choose any other, and these take the place of those who have died, in order that their number may be always maintained.

These knights know the things of their religion, but the others know nothing of them; they content themselves with saying that they believe what their knights believe.

The knights take the virginity of all the young maidens; only after one of them has done with a maiden may her father, or the knight, wed her to whom he pleases.

But before they lie with them they fatten them with milk until their skin is bursting like the skin of a fig, because they hold that the thin maidens are not so good as the fat. They say that the belly of the fat maidens is enlarged, and that they are able to engender great sons. And when the maiden has become fat she is shown all naked to the knight who is to take her, and he then declares to her father that she is fat enough. And the father and mother make her go into the sea for a certain time each day, so that she may lose the surplus of fat; and she is then led to the knight, and after he has taken her virginity her parents lead her back to their house.

Their manner of fighting consists in hurling stones, without other weapons beside a short staff for striking. They are very valiant and brave warriors; their soil has very many stones, and they well defend their country.

They wear no raiment; only the coloured palm-leaves which take the place of breeches and conceal their sex; but for the most part they go quite naked. They have no gold or silver, nor any money, nor jewels, nor anything else artificial, save that which they make with the stones that serve them as knives, and so they build the houses in which they live.

They disdain gold, silver, and all other metals, making mock of those that desire them; and in general there are none of them whose opinion is different. No quality of cloth pleases them, and they make mock of those who desire it, as they do in respect of gold and silver and the other things of which I spoke. But they greatly value iron, which they work with their stones, and of this they make hooks for fishing.

They have wheat and oats, but they have no skill to make bread; they make flour of them, which they eat with meat and butter.

They have very many fig-trees and dragon-trees,

and dates, but no good ones, and herbs which they eat. And they have sheep, goats, and swine in plenty.

They shave themselves with stones. Some there are that call themselves Christians; and after the Infante had sent thither Dom Fernando de Castro with his fleet, in which were two thousand five hundred men and seventy horses, many of these Canarians became Christians; and they were not all conquered, because Dom Fernando feared that he would lack supplies. When the Infante wished to send his people there again the King of Castile opposed it, saying that the island was his conquest, which was not true; and it was for this reason that an enterprise so virtuous as that of leading these people to the law of Jesus Christ was not brought to a successful end. This fleet was sent in the year of Christ 1424.

The inhabitants of this island believe that it is a great wrong to slaughter cattle and flay them; and if they can get a Christian from outside they are right glad to make of him their butcher; and when they cannot get Christians to ply this trade they seek for the worst men of the island, and put this task upon them. And the women will have nought to do with the butchers, and the men do not eat with them, for they hold them in worse horror than we hold the leprous.

They make fire by rubbing two pieces of wood one against the other.

The women dislike giving the breast to their children; for which reason most of the children are suckled by the goats.

· · ·

The men of the island of Gomera make war with

wands, which are sharpened and burned with fire, and have the appearance of arrows. They are altogether naked and without covering, of which they have no shame. They make a mock at all garments, saying that they are but bags in which men tie themselves up.

They have no corn but oats, and of this only a little; also they have swine and goats. They make their meals in general of milk and herbs, like the beasts; with the roots of rushes, and little meat. They eat things unclean and disgusting, such as rats, fleas, lice, and ticks, and they hold these to be good food.

They have no houses, but live in caves or huts.

Their women are, so to say, in common. When one of them goes to the house of another the latter forthwith gives him his wife in token of hospitality; and if he does not do so, this is taken in bad part; and for this reason the sons do not inherit from their father, but only the nephews, the sons of their sisters.

They pass the greater part of their time in singing and dancing, because their vice is to enjoy without labour. Their supreme happiness they find in fornication, for they have no knowledge of the law; they believe only in God.

They have seven hundred warriors, who have a duke and certain chiefs.

.   .   .

It seems to me that the life of the inhabitants of the Isle of Hell or Teneriffe is better, for these have wheat, oats, and vegetables in plenty, also many swine, sheep, and goats, and they array themselves in the skins of beasts. But they have no houses, dwelling in caves or huts.

. . .

. . . Their weapons are made of the hearts of pine-trees; they are like great darts, very sharp, grilled over the fire. They are eight thousand, divided into nine bands, and each band has its king, whom they have always with them, even if he dies, until the other king who replaces him dies in his turn; so that always they have one dead and one living king. And when the second king dies, and they have two dead kings, and they have to rid themselves of one of them, in accordance with their brutish custom they take the body and cast it away; and he who carries the dead man on his back says, when he throws his body away, that he is sending him to his salvation.

These men are strong and hardy, and each has his wife; they live more like human beings than those of the other islands. They fight against one another, which is their chief care. They believe in a God.

. . .

The inhabitants of the island of Palma have neither wheat nor vegetables; only sheep and milk and grasses, and this is their food.

They do not acknowledge God, and have no faith; but they believe that they have one. They are very brutish.

There are men among them whom they call kings. Their weapons are like to those of Teneriffe, but they set upon the point of their darts a sharpened horn, and another horn at the other end, but not so sharp.

They do not eat fish; while in all the other islands

the inhabitants devise means of taking fish and eat them, these neither take fish nor eat of them.

They have five hundred men; it is truly a great marvel that being so free they have never been conquered since the beginning of the world; which proves that all things are as God wills that they shall be during the time and within the limits that are pleasing to Him.

. . .

In Chapter v of this book I spoke, among other things which the Infante had performed in the service of God, of his peopling of the isles of Madeira and other islands of these parts. I wish now to relate how these islands were peopled; all the more as I have now spoken of the Canary Isles.

In the household of the Infante there were two noble squires reared by that lord, two young gentlemen of great merit.[1] When the Infante returned from Ceuta after overcoming the power of the Moorish kings these two gentlemen besought that the Infante would employ them in such a manner that they might increase the honour of their names, like men who desired it greatly, for it seemed to them that their time was ill employed if they were not labouring to do some good thing.

The Infante, marking their goodwill, caused a barque to be armed for them, in which they were to set forth to fight against the Moors, and sail in quest of the Land of Guinea, the search for which this prince had already in his mind.[2] And God wishing

[1] João Gonçalves Zarco and Tristão Vaz.

[2] We see that the Infante had the discovery of Guinea in mind from the very outset of the expeditions which he despatched. On this point Azurara differs slightly from Cadomosto.

to do so much good to this realm, as also to other countries, He guided the voyage of these two young lords in such fashion that having had to struggle against tempests, they came to the island which is to-day called Porto Santo, which is near the Isle of Madeira, and measures nigh upon seven leagues in compass.

They remained there for some days, and having well considered this land, it seemed to them that there would be great profit in peopling it. On returning to the kingdom they spoke of this to the Infante, telling him of the good quality of the soil, and their desire to people it, which pleased this prince greatly. He straightway commanded that those things of which the two gentlemen should have need in order to return to this island should be given to them.

While they were thus employed in these preparations a *fidalgo* belonging to the household of the Infante Dom João, who was called Bartholomeu Perestrello, joined them, and so soon as all was in readiness they set forth together for this island.

Now it happened that among the things which they took with them to set loose upon the island was a doe rabbit which had been given to Bartholomeu Perestrello by a friend; she was with young, and they kept her in a cage; she littered during the voyage, and on reaching the island they took her ashore with her little ones.

Having built their cabins and commenced their labours, they set the rabbit and her little ones at liberty, so that they might breed. And they bred so well that ere long they filled all the island, and the men could sow nothing which was not immediately devoured or spoiled. This was truly a thing astonishing, for in the following year when they came to the island they killed vast numbers of these rabbits, but this killing made not the smallest difference. And for this reason they abandoned that island and went to the other, the Isle of Madeira, which measures forty leagues in compass and is twelve leagues distant from Porto Santo. The two gentlemen, João Gonçalves and Tristão, remained there, and Bartholomeu Perestrello returned to the kingdom.

They found that this second island had excellent soil, and much water, which could readily be led whither it was required for watering the land; they began to sow the soil, and they had very good crops from it. The air on the island was good and wholesome, and there were many birds there, which at first they were able to take with their hands, and they quickly found many other advantages on this island.

They gave tidings of all these things to the Infante, who straightway set to work to send other men thither, and the things proper to the Church, with its priests, so that in a very short time a great part of this island was cultivated.

And the Infante, considering the merit of these two men, and that they were the cause of its peopling, gave them the government of the island. João Gonçalves Zarco was a nobleman, and had been knighted at the siege of Tangier in a battle which was won by the Infante on a Friday (of which there is somewhat said in the chronicle of the realm, with more particulars), and this João Gonçalves Zarco had already distinguished himself on many other occasions, especially at Ceuta, in the victory over the Moors on the day of arriving there; and to him the Infante gave the government of the island in that part of it which is called Funchal. And he gave to Tristão the government of the other part of the island, which is called Machico. This Tristão had been knighted at Ceuta; he was a valiant man, but not so noble in all other things as João Gonçalves Zarco.

This island began to be peopled in the year of Jesus Christ 1420; and at the time when this history was written it was already moderately well peopled, for there were one hundred and fifty inhabitants, without counting the merchants, unmarried men and women, newly born children, priests and monks, and other persons who came and went by reason of their merchandise and other affairs of the island.

In the year 1445 the Infante despatched a knight who was called Gonçalo Velho, Commander of the Order of Christ, with instructions to people two other islands which lie 170 leagues to the north-west of Madeira.

It was the Infante Dom Pedro who began to people one of these islands, with the consent of his brother; but the death of this Infante soon followed, so that the Infante Dom Henrique continued his work. Dom Pedro had given this island the name of San Miguel, since he had a special devotion for this saint.[1]

---

[1] On the chart made by VALSEQUA in Majorca in the year 1439 (unpublished) the following note is inscribed in the midst of the Azores: *These islands were discovered by Diogo de Senill, pilot of the King of Portugal, in the year 1432.*

We transcribe this note because of the date and the name of the pilot, for the date agrees with that given by P. Freire in his *Vie de l'enfant Dom Henrique* (pp. 319–20), who states that the island of Santa Maria

The Infante sent once more to the island of Porto Santo, Bartholomeu Perestrello, he who had gone thither first with João Gonçalves Zarco and Tristão; and he instructed him to people it. But the multitude of rabbits there is such that nothing can be cultivated there; but many flocks and herds are grazed there, and the gum of the dragon-tree is gathered there, which is sold in this realm and in other countries.

The Infante also caused sheep to be released upon another island which lies seven leagues from Madeira, with the intention of peopling it like the rest; it is called *Deserta*, the desert isle.

Of these seven islands[1] four are as large as the island of Madeira, and the other three are smaller.

The better to favour the Order of Christ, of which he was at this time the Governor, the Infante Dom Henrique gave this Order full spiritual power over

des Açores was discovered by Gonçalo Velho, not by Diogo de Senill, as VALSEQUA states.

Dr. Murr, in his dissertation on the globe of MARTIN DE BOHÈME or DE BEHAIM, also states that the Azores were discovered in 1432. However, there is little agreement among the writers of the century as to the true date of their discovery. And if we compare the charts made before the year 1432 with what Freire says (p. 323) concerning the discovery of the island of San Miguel—namely, that the existence of this island (according to the statement of the Infante Dom Henrique) *was in agreement with his old charts*, it would seem that the Azores were discovered before the year 1432.

As a matter of fact, these islands are marked in the Parma chart, which is of the fourteenth century; and in the Catalan chart in the Bibliothèque de Paris these islands are denoted also by Italian names, three of which are those given to them by the Portuguese. It is interesting to note that in the Majorca chart (although it is more modern) the names of these islands have been altered, while in the Catalan chart, which is sixty-four years older, as in the Italian charts of the fifteenth century, we read the names given by the Portuguese navigators: Corvo, S. Jorge, Santa Maria.

[1] The Azores. There are nine islands.

the islands of Madeira and Porto Santo, and full
spiritual and temporal power over the other island,
of which he appointed Gonçalo Velho commander,
and also of the island of San Miguel, surrendering to
the Order the tithe and the moiety of the sugars.

. . .

. . .

It was in the year 1446 that the Infante began to
make ready his ships for the conquest of the Canary
Isles, but before he organized this undertaking he
requested the Infante Dom Pedro, his brother, who
at this time was governing the realm in the King's
name, to grant him a charter by which all natives of
the kingdom would be forbidden to go to the Canaries
to make war or to traffic in merchandise without the
authority of the said Infante. This charter was granted
him, and further, he was given the right to take the
fifth part of all things that might be brought from
the islands; which was very just, considering the great
disbursements which this noble prince had already
made in respect of their conquest.

. . .

After this conquest, which has already been recorded, incursions were made by Portuguese ships for
the purpose of carrying off captives from the Canaries.
The Kings of Castile complained of these incursions,
and there were many disputes between Portugal and
Castile concerning the possession of these islands,[1]
which afterwards became finally Spanish.

[1] LAS CASAS, in his *History of the Indies*, deals at length with this
question, especially in chapter viii.

CHAPTER IX

*The death of Nuno Tristão. The west coast of Africa
discovered as far as Sierra Leone and beyond. First
commercial ventures*

THE author records the death of Nuno Tristão.
This knight, reared from early childhood in the
household of the Infante, deeply devoted to this
prince, and aware of his increasing desire to learn
more concerning the western coast of Africa, resolved
to return thither. He had been one of the first to
make this adventurous voyage; and now that men
had discovered the Nile of the Negroes and gone
beyond it, he desired once more to set forth, and if
possible to go farther still.

. . .

. . . And having passed Cape Verde, he sailed
still sixty leagues beyond this cape, until he beheld
the mouth of a river; and on its banks he thought to
find a few villages. He lowered two boats into the sea,
in which two and twenty men took their place, ten
in one, twelve in another. They ascended the river;
and the rising tide aiding them, they rowed in the
direction of some houses which they saw upon the
right bank.

Before they came to land from the other bank came
twelve boats containing seventy to eighty *Guineus*, all
black, and holding bows. And as the tide rose one of
these boats reached the other bank (before the
Portuguese) and landed the negroes whom it had
brought, and who forthwith began to shoot arrows
at those who were in the ships' boats. And the negroes

who were in the other boats hastened to come down upon ours, and immediately they were near enough they began to launch against them their accursed and envenomed weapons. In this fashion they followed them until they reached the caravel, which was at sea, beyond the mouth of the river. Our men reached it at length, but they were all wounded, and four died immediately even in the boats.

Although wounded, they made their boats fast to the caravel, and began to make ready to depart, seeing the danger in which they stood; but they could not weigh the anchors by reason of the arrows which fell upon them in such numbers, and they had perforce to cut the cables; and they had no anchor left. They began immediately to make sail, but they had to abandon the boats, for they could not hoist them aboard while the arrows were falling on them.

Of the twenty-two men who had gone shorewards two alone survived, Andrea Dias and Alvaro da Costa, both squires of the Infante, and natives of the town of Evora; and the nineteen others died, for the poison was so skilfully compounded that the smallest wound sufficed to inflict death. And there too died that noble knight Nuno Tristão,[1] very desirous to live longer, for he had not had time to purchase his death as he would have wished . . .

In all there were one and twenty dead, for of the seven men who had remained in the caravel two were wounded as they were striving to lift the anchor. But how to work the ship and continue her voyage, and how escape from these accursed people? The two

[1] This river was called the *Rio de Tristão* or *Rio de Nuno Tristão*, and is so marked in almost all the old charts, in memory of this catastrophe.

squires who were left, as we have said, did not wholly avoid this peril, for being wounded they came very near to death, and with this sickness they were prostrate for twenty days, nor could they in any wise aid the others who were striving to work the caravel, and of whom there were but five; a ship-boy knowing little indeed of the art of navigating, a very young man of the Infante's household, who was called Ayres Tinoco, and had been engaged as clerk (of the expedition), and a young *Guineu* who had been taken with the first captives carried off from this country; and further, two boys, quite young, who were living with certain of the squires dead in this adventure.

Of a truth we must feel pity when we think of the difficulties, pains, and perils which they had to overcome during this voyage.

They wept and lamented the death of such a captain, and of the others, their comrades and their friends; they dreaded the abominable enemies whom they felt to be so close upon them, whose arrows had mortally wounded in so short a time such men, and in numbers so great; and above all they had right feeble means of salvation. For the ship-boy in whom they had all put their hope confessed plainly his little knowledge, saying that he could not steer the ship nor do anything profitable in the art of navigating, except as he was commanded; but that he would do all that he was ordered to do!

O great and supreme succour of all those that are disabled and distressed, Thou who dost never abandon those that call on Thee in their affliction, Thou didst hear the cries of those whose lamentations ascended toward Thee, and who, their eyes uplifted toward the clouds, entreated Thee to succour them! Thou didst give strength and skill to a very young boy, born and reared at Olivença, which is a town in the heart of the realm, very far from the sea; inspired by divine grace, he piloted the ship, commanding the ship-boy to proceed directly northwards, veering somewhat to the Levant of the wind which is called north-east, for he thought that in this direction they would find the Kingdom of Portugal which they so desired to attain!

The vessel thus proceeding upon its way, and a portion of the day having already elapsed, they went to look at Nuno Tristão and the others who were wounded; and they had perforce to cast them into the sea . . .

· · ·

. . . This boy was that Ayres Tinoco of whom I have already spoken; in him God placed so much of His grace that for two months he piloted the caravel; nevertheless, all had doubts of the end of such a voyage, for during these two months they never had sight of land. At length, after this lapse of time, they perceived an armed flatboat, of which they were in great dread, believing it to be Moorish. But when they knew that it belonged to a Galician corsair who was called Pero Falcão they were filled with joy, and still more when these men advised them that they were off the coast of Portugal, not far from a place which was called Sines (in the province of Algarve).

And so they came to Lagos, and immediately presented themselves to the Infante, to whom they recounted the sad events of their voyage, giving him a great quantity of the arrows which had slain their companions. The Infante was deeply grieved by this loss, since he had reared almost all these men in his house; and although he believed firmly in the salvation of their souls, he could not refrain from lamenting the death of those who for years had lived beside him. And like a good seigneur, having comprehended that they had died in his service, he took particular care of their wives and children.

. . .

João Gonçalves Zarco, captain of the Isle of Madeira, not being content with the result of this expedition, which he had sent into Guinea in the service of his lord the Infante Dom Henrique, resolved to send thither a second caravel, commanded, like the first, by his nephew Alvaro Fernandes; recommending him to go as far as he could go, and to do his utmost to bring back to the prince some booty whose novelty and magnificence should bear witness to his desire to do his lord good service.

The caravel sailed in one stage to Cape Verde, and then to Cabo dos Matos, where they sent their boat ashore in the hope of making some capture. They found some negroes, with whom they fought. Alvaro Fernandes killed a negro chief, and took his lance and his buckler, which he carried back to the Infante with other things; and they took two women and a child. And one of the negresses was so lusty that three men had great difficulty in dragging her along.

And they found on the bank the droppings of elephants, of which the bulk, according to those that saw them, was "of the bigness of a man's body."

They continued their voyage southward, and they saw a river[1] which they ascended in their boat. They

---

[1] On the chart of JUAN DE LA COSA (1500) this is marked with the name *Rio de Lagos*; on that of JOÃO FREIRE (1546) and others with the name *Rio de Lago*. In DOURADO's chart this river is shown to the south of Cabos dos Matos, but without a name.

found some houses, from which they brought one woman to the caravel. Then they returned thither with the intention of going farther. As they ascended the course of the river in their boat, of a sudden four or five boats filled with negroes came down upon them. Not wishing to give them battle, seeing that they were superior in numbers and were armed with poisoned arrows, they turned about. However, one of the negroes' boats came to within bowshot of them. And the captain Alvares Fernandes was hurt in the leg with one of their arrows. Since he was not taken unawares, he immediately tore out the arrow and washed the wound with wine and oil, and rubbed it with treacle; thus he escaped death, but was very near it.

Nevertheless, those of the caravel, although their captain lay grievously sick, continued to sail southward until they came to a sandy headland which protected a wide bay; into this they went in their small boat, hoping to explore the country at this point. But they beheld on the bank some hundred and twenty Guineus with lances, bucklers, and bows who were making toward them. And on coming down to the beach they began to sing and to dance, as though to show how little they made of those who were in the boat.

"*Not wishing to accept their invitation to this festival,*" the Portuguese returned to the caravel.

This sandy headland and this bay lie southward 110 leagues from Cape Verde.[1] And it was this caravel that went farthest that year.

. . .

The tidings of the death of Nuno Tristão and his companions, and the knowledge of the terrible danger of these poisoned arrows, did nothing to damp the

---

[1] The wide bay which they found 110 leagues to the south of Cape Verde lies beyond Sierra Leone, and is marked on the charts of JUAN DE LA COSA (1500), FREIRE (1546), and VAZ DOURADO.

spirits of navigators so desirous of winning glory, and serving the Infante Dom Henrique, whose generous rewards increased their zeal.

This year seven caravels left Lagos all together, and in accordance with the custom established by the Infante they laid in supplies at the Isle of Madeira; and from this island two other ships joined the caravels from Portugal. One of these was equipped by Tristão Vaz, and the other was commanded by Garcia Homen, the son-in-law of João Gonçalves Zarco.

They sought without success to make some captures on the Canaries in passing, and they sailed sixty leagues beyond Cape Verde, where they found a wide river,[1] which they entered with their caravels. One of these, however, equipped by the Bishop of Algarve, ran aground upon a sandbank and could not be got off. The crew and all their supplies were transferred to the other ships.

Some of the men landed and marched some distance into the interior. They did not find any of the natives, who had departed elsewhere, but they saw large areas of land sown with crops, and many cotton-trees and others, and rice-fields.

Some of the men halted there and rested; others ventured farther; Diogo Affonso and fifteen companions, among whom was a certain João Villas, a youth of the Infante's household, who was engaged as clerk. These men having entered a very dense wood, of a sudden the *Guineus* fell upon their flank, rising up out of the thick brush, with their short lances and their bucklers. These negroes were very numerous, and they wounded seven of our men, of whom five died at once, poisoned by their arrows.

The other Portuguese, who had been left in the rear, came to the rescue of their companions, and with much difficulty, by sheer courage, they succeeded in escaping from a position of great danger.

[1] The Rio Grande.

After this, as their ships were overloaded with the crew and the supplies of the Bishop's caravel, they returned to Portugal without going farther.

On the return voyage they again attempted to make some captures on the Canaries, but after risking their lives in skirmishes with the natives they succeeded in bringing off only two women.

. . .

In the year 1446 Gomes Pires, the captain of whom we have already spoken, remembered what he had said to the Moors of the Rio do Ouro the previous year: that they must wait at this point a year later with negroes and other merchandise.

Having asked leave of the Infante, he set out with two caravels, one of which was decked, while the other was only a fishing-boat; between the two there were twenty men and Gomes Pires.

Having put in at Madeira to obtain supplies, one of the caravels, sailing before the other, went to the *Rio do Ouro*, which it ascended for a distance of six leagues, until it came to a harbour, Porto da Caldeira, which the Portuguese had visited before.

Then they lit great fires to attract the attention of the Moors, who presently came to meet them. Gomes Pires asked them to bring him negroes, saying that he would give cloth in exchange. The Moors replied:

". . . We are not merchants, and there are none about here. They are inland, exchanging their merchandise. If they knew that you were here they would do their best to join you, for these men have many *Guineus*, as well as gold, and other things which would please you."[1] . . .

. . .

[1] This passage shows that before the discovery of the Rio do Ouro by the Portuguese there had been no trading with Europeans in this neighbourhood.

We see, in fact, that the Arabs were well aware that the caravans

Gomes Pires endeavoured to persuade the Moors to send someone to advise the merchants that he was waiting on the Rio do Ouro. They accepted the price offered for this commission, but did not undertake the journey.

In the meantime the other caravel reached the Rio do Ouro. Gomes Pires, seeing that the Moors were trifling with him, told them that their bond of friendship was broken, and that they must now defend themselves.

And having undertaken a few dangerous expeditions into the interior, they made some prisoners, whom they carried on board their caravels.

During this voyage Gomes Pires remained one and twenty days at the *Porto da Caldeira*, which is situated, as we have said, six leagues from the mouth of the river (*Rio do Ouro*), in order to establish commercial relations, but his efforts were not successful. He then went four leagues farther along the other bank, and saw the island which lies in the river.[1] And having covered in all eleven leagues, they came into conflict with the Moors, who took refuge *"among the very tall rocks which are found in this neighbourhood."*

These rocks are the *Seven Mountains* which the Portuguese navigators marked on their charts, and which are already indicated on the Mappamundi of Fra Mouro (1457–9), copied from the Portuguese nautical charts; they are the *"High Mountains"* of Martin Behaim's globe.

. . .

could not come to the Rio do Ouro without making several journeys across the desert, and that they would not be inclined to risk such an effort for an uncertain result, preferring to keep to their customary routes and their old trading stations.

The voyage of Gomes Pires, although unfruitful, marks one of the first steps towards the maritime trade of Portugal, which afterwards underwent rapid development and assumed enormous proportions.

[1] Marked as *"ilot de roches très élevé"* on Admiral Roussin's chart.

The following year, which was the year 1447 after the birth of Jesus Christ, the Infante, seeing that the Moors of the Rio do Ouro did not desire to open negotiations for the exchange of any merchandise (and even if they had harboured any such desire, it was greatly diminished by the fact that Gomes Pires had made captives there), wished to make an attempt to establish this commerce with the Moors at a place which is called Meça,[1] and at the same time to explore this region more fully, and obtain knowledge of it.

He equipped the caravel of one of his squires, who was called Diogo Gil, a man who had served him well in the war against the Moors, by sea as well as on land. And the preparations being thus in hand, the Prince had intelligence that a merchant of Castile, Marcos Cisfontes by name, had twenty-six captive Moors from this part who were already ransomed against a certain number of *Guineus*. In order that his ship should have a reason (apparent) for making this voyage, the Infante made it known to the merchant that if he so desired his Moors should be taken to Meça in this caravel, on the condition that he should give to the Infante a certain portion of the profit of the ransom.

In truth it was not so much the hope of gain in this affair that moved the Infante, but two other reasons: the first, that he would thus have a better chance of learning more of this country; and the second, that they would bring back some *Guineus*, and he hoped to make them embrace the faith of Christ.[2]

[1] Messa, a town in the province of Sus in Morocco.
[2] This shows us that at this time the trade in Guinea negroes was

The merchant was well content with this proposal of the Infante's; soon the caravel was armed, and having taken on its cargo it sailed for Meça, where there was much parley, which led to no result.

"If you so desire," said the squire João Fernandes, who, as you already know, sojourned seven months among the Moors of the Sahara, "I myself will go ashore, and I will undertake this ransom." He spoke thus to Diogo Gil, the captain, to Rodrigo Eannes, another squire whom the Infante had sent out to engage in this affair, and to a Castilian merchant who was to have negotiated the ransom.

Then João Fernandes, having obtained his warranties, went among the Moors, with whom he parleyed in such wise that he had brought to the caravel *fifty Guineus* against eighteen Moors who were delivered to them.[1]

It came to pass that the wind began to blow so strongly from the south that the caravel had to make sail forthwith and take the homeward way. On this voyage they took back to the Infante a lion, which he afterwards sent to a place in Ireland called Galway, to one of his servants who dwelt in that country, because it was known that such an animal had never

still carried on through the ports lying to the north of *Cabo Nao*. The Infante knew, before entering upon these negotiations, that hereabouts there was one of the centres of trade between Morocco and the negro states.

[1] This passage proves the influence which João Fernandes had over the Moors, doubtless because he spoke Arabic and had lived among them. M. EYRIEZ, in a biographical article on this intrepid traveller (*Biographie universelle*), states that he was the first European to penetrate the interior of Africa, and that the details of his narrative have many analogies with the narrative of MUNGO PARK.

been seen there. And João Fernandes remained on shore, until another ship came to seek him . . .

. . .

This same year Antão Gonçalves returned to the Rio do Ouro, his mission being to persuade the Moors to exchange their merchandise. But in vain. The Moors laid an ambush for him, in which he all but lost his life, and one of his men was slain there.

Another caravel went the same year to the Rio do Ouro, bringing back oil and seal pelts.

. . .

The fame of these events having spread throughout the world, it reached the Court of the King of Denmark, Sweden, and Norway; and as you know that noble men are always moved to seek these adventures, it came to pass that a gentleman of the household of this prince, desirous of seeing the world, obtained leave to visit our realm.

Having dwelt for some time in the household of the Infante, he besought him one day to cause a caravel to be equipped for him, and to allow him to go to the Land of the Negroes. The Infante, ever ready to aid valiant men desirous of increasing their honour and their goods, forthwith caused a caravel to be equipped in the best possible manner; and he charged this gentleman to go to Cape Verde, and endeavour to obtain a warranty from the king of that country, for he had heard tell that he was a puissant lord; he gave him letters to be presented to this king, and charged him to declare to him, on his behalf, matters bearing upon the service of God and His holy faith. This because he had been assured that this king was a Christian; and the conclusion of all this was that if this report was true, the Infante requested their king to aid him in the war against the Moors of Africa, in which the King Dom Affonso, who was then reigning in Portugal, as well as himself and his vassals, was engaged.

All was ready ere long; and this foreign squire, who was called Vallarte, embarked in the ship, as also a knight of the Order of Christ, Fernando Affonso by name, a servant of the Infante, and reared by him, whom the Infante was sending in this caravel because Vallarte was a stranger, and was not sufficiently familiar with the usages and customs of these people to have the command of mariners and give the word in other matters relating to navigation; thus Fernando Affonso went almost as an ambassador in case they attained to having speech of this king; and he took with him two native interpreters of this country (Cape Verde). But the captain in chief was Vallarte.

Thus they set forth, and had to contend against great tempests, and only after six months had elapsed did they reach the Isle of Palma, which is in the Land of the Negroes, not far from Cape Verde. There they took counsel as to what they would now do in accordance with the commands of the Infante; and they set sail anew and went farther, for they had not yet come to the harbour which they were seeking.

When they came to the cape, to a place called Abram, they dropped their boat into the sea and went ashore, Vallarte and some others. They found there already a number of Moors; and Vallarte asked that he should be given one, and he would give another in exchange, during their parleys, as hostage. They declared to him that they could not do this without the order of a knight who was called Guitenya, and who was in this place as governor. He, so soon as he had word of Vallarte's offer, came to him and granted his request . . .

Much parleying followed. Fernando Affonso gave this chief one of the letters of the Infante, which he caused to be interpreted to him, explaining that it was his mission to speak to his king. But the Moorish chief replied that the king was very far away, and was at this time engaged in a war against one of his vassals; and Fernando Affonso could declare to him what it was that he wished to say. Other chiefs coming up, the conversation became confused. The Moors on this coast were so many and so curious that by pressing round the chiefs who were engaged in parley they made all converse impossible.

In the end the Moors promised to send a message to their king, Boor, to ask him to come and speak with the envoys of the Portuguese king.

In the meantime the chiefs sent presents to the captains of the caravel: the best food which they had, goats, kids, conserves, butter, flour, corn, milk, palm wine, and other things, such as elephants' teeth. They were given presents in exchange: above all, cloths and other wares.

One day the Portuguese asked the chief Guitenya if he could not procure for them a dead elephant, so that they might take its skin, teeth, and bones; they promised him in exchange "a tent in tissue of linen in which twenty-five to thirty men could shelter, yet so light that a single man could carry it on his shoulders."

This chief being gone to hunt the elephant which they demanded, Vallarte wished one day to go ashore, and despite the advice of his companions he persisted in this desire.

.   .   .

. . . And as the boat was already near the shore a negro came towards them with a calabash filled with wine, making as though he would give it them. Vallarte commanded those who were rowing to go closer; they begged him once more not to do this, but they had to obey him; and this to the misfortune of all, for the canoe having approached the shore, a movement of the rowers ran it aground. At this moment Vallarte was regarding a group of negroes who were squatting in the shade of a tree; the negro interpreter who was in the boat, on leaning over as though he would take the calabash, let it slip into the water.

Seeing this those in the boat wished to return to the caravel; but a wave cast them on the shore. Immediately the negroes ran all together upon the boat, casting their spears. In such sort that of all those who had left the caravel on this expedition only one escaped, by swimming. But of the others it was not known what was their end, for he who returned to the caravel related that he had seen only one slain; and that having looked back twice or thrice while escaping, he saw Vallarte still seated in the bows of the boat.

However, at the time of our writing this history some native captives of this country were brought before the Infante, and they related that there was a castle in the interior, very far from the coast, in which there were four Christians, one of whom was dead; but that the other three were still living; and according to the indications given by these captives, many believed that these Christians must be Vallarte and his companions.

Fernando Affonso, greatly moved by this unhappy event, and having no longer a boat in which he could go ashore, weighed anchor and returned to the kingdom.[1]

Affonso records the number of natives brought from Africa to Portugal from the beginning of the Infante's expeditions to the year 1448:

. . . The souls of the Infidels who came hither from these countries, thanks to the virtue and skill of our glorious prince; which, I have found in counting them, were 924, of whom the greater number, as I

---

[1] This passage is rather important, for it explains the event recorded in the letter of *Antoniotto Usus di Mare*, or rather, *Antoine da Nole*, dated December 12, 1455, found in the Genoese archives by Graberg in 1802 (*Annali di geografia e di statistica*, vol. ii, p. 285), in which this traveller states that he met in these parts a countryman of his whom he believed to be a member of the expedition of Vivaldi (which had set out 170 years earlier!) and of which, according to the Italian authors, no news had ever been received.

It is not admissible that a descendant of a member of the expedition of Genoese galleys of *Thedisio Doria* and *Vivaldi* could have retained the white complexion and the language of his ancestor. Antoine da Nole cannot have seen, in this region, any white man other than the sailors of the Portuguese caravel commanded by Fernando Affonso and Vallarte; all the more as none of the Portuguese captains, nor Cadomosto either, ever found, on any part of the African coast beyond Cape Bojador, vestiges or traditions which pointed to Europeans anterior to the Portuguese discoveries.

Of Vivaldi's expedition nothing was ever heard after his departure in the thirteenth century. In Antoine da Nole's day there were only traditions; the expedition had set out with the intention of passing through the Straits of Gibraltar in order to make a voyage into the unknown in the direction of the Ponent. Da Nole, influenced by these traditions, and knowing that a white Christian had been seen in this region of Africa, imagined that he might be a descendant of some member of Vivaldi's expedition, which had set out nearly two centuries earlier. He certainly cannot have heard of Vallarte's voyage, which took place only eight years previously. We must remember, too, that foreigners were sometimes to be found in the crews of the Portuguese caravels of this period.

have already said, were converted to the true path of the faith . . .

. . . And because it seems to us that this volume is already something large, we shall conclude it here, with the intention of writing another, extending to the conclusion of the Infante's work; although that which came to pass afterwards did not call for such effort and fatigue; since from this date all matters relative to these countries were effected much rather by the means of negotiation, and exchanges of merchandise, than by the force of arms . . .

OVERLEAF

particulars of publications
of similar interest
issued by

GEORGE ALLEN & UNWIN LTD
LONDON: 40 MUSEUM STREET, W.C.1
LEIPZIG: (F. VOLCKMAR) HOSPITALSTR. 10
CAPE TOWN: 73 ST. GEORGE'S STREET
TORONTO: 91 WELLINGTON STREET, WEST
BOMBAY: 15 GRAHAM ROAD, BALLARD ESTATE
WELLINGTON, N.Z.: 8 KINGS CRESCENT, LOWER HUTT
SYDNEY, N.S.W.: AUSTRALIA HOUSE, WYNYARD SQUARE

Those Were Good Days

by CARL LUDWIG SCHLEICH

TRANSLATED BY BERNARD MIALL

Demy 8vo.   *Illustrated*   12s. 6d. net

The reminiscences of Carl Ludwig Schleich, a distinguished if somewhat heretical surgeon and pathologist, and the pioneer of local anaesthesia, who was also a brilliant musician and painter, and a writer of great originality, should make interesting and unusual reading. Schleich was the intimate friend of Strindberg, to whom he devotes a revealing chapter, the pupil and assistant of the great Virchow, and a friend of Paul Ehrlich. A Pomeranian, the son of a Stettin physician, of whom he paints an unforgettable picture, Schleich was a true citizen of the "old Germany" of poets, musicians, philosophers, and scientists which has always enjoyed the respect and affection of the civilized world: but there was something individual, irrepressible, and lawless in this little Pomeranian surgeon which will endear him to English readers. His autobiography contains a delightful record of a happy and untrammelled childhood, a description of riotous rather than studious years at several universities, the history of an unusual and somewhat troubled career, and a number of valuable portraits of men whose names are household words.

365,000 copies sold in Germany

Brahms: His Life and Work

by KARL GEIRINGER

Demy 8vo.   *Illustrated*   10s. 6d. net

The great importance of this new biography of Brahms lies in the fact that the author has had access to a large quantity of letters, hitherto unavailable and which throw new light on the character and genius of the master and on the contemporary scene.

The book is divided into two parts, the biography proper and a critical section in which each category of the master's compositions is considered separately; a final chapter treats of Brahms's character as a man and artist.

It is a fascinating study, the value of which will be fully appreciated by all music lovers.

Zaharoff, the Armaments King

by ROBERT NEUMANN

Demy 8vo.   TRANSLATED BY R. T. CLARK   10s. 6d. net

Sir Basil Zaharoff is still one of the mystery men of Europe. Was he a mere unscrupulous adventurer, a modern pirate, a humble member of a formidable conspiracy against the peace of Europe, or a high-souled patriot using what instruments offered him for the benefit of his country? And if so what country? Is this member of the British Knightage a Greek, Jew, or Rumanian. Was what he was credited with doing his own work or was he a tool of secret interests! What, in fact, did he do and is he doing? Herr Robert Neumann has persistently tracked down every ascertainable fact and, so far as the investigator can, stripped the falsehood away. The result is to lose some of the mystery and gain more, because under the investigator's microscope Zaharoff seems a greater enigma than ever.

Emil Ludwig has said: "Neumann's book is an indictment at a high level. . . . I only regret that it is not given away for all to read."

LONDON: GEORGE ALLEN & UNWIN LIMITED